Fighting Chan

A Play

N. J. Crisp

Samuel French – London
New York – Sydney – Toronto – Hollywood

FIGHTING CHANCE

First presented in London, at the Apollo Theatre, by Bill Kenwright, in association with the Thorndike Theatre, Leatherhead on 8th August, 1985, with the following cast:

Physiotherapist	Joyce Rae
Tony	Brian Marshall
Len	Victor Maddern
Douglas	Lewis Jones
Philip	Simon Williams
Kathy	Elizabeth Quinn
Speech Therapist	Penny Brownjohn
Nurse	Kate Dunn
Ken	Robin McDonald

Directed by Roger Clissold
Designed by Stuart Stanley

The play takes place in a residential rehabilitation centre for neurological patients, near London, and is based on the author's experience as a patient in 1976 and for a shorter period in 1982

Time—the present

ACT I

Scene 1	Gymnasium	9.40 a.m. Monday	Philip's Week 1
Scene 2	Speech Therapy	2.30. p.m. Tuesday	Week 2
Scene 3	Room 6	5.30 p.m. Wednesday	Week 3
Scene 4	Physiotherapy	10.00 a.m. Thursday	Week 3
Scene 5	Patients' Lounge	9.00 p.m. Thursday	Week 4

ACT II

Scene 1	Room 6	7.30 a.m. Monday	Week 5
Scene 2	Patients' Lounge	9.30 p.m. Thursday	Week 6
Scene 3	Speech Therapy	2.15 p.m. Monday	Week 7
Scene 4	Physiotherapy	3.30 p.m. Tuesday	Week 7
Scene 5	Patients' Lounge	6.45 p.m. Monday	The Last Week
Scene 6	Gymnasium	9.40 a.m. Friday	The Last Week

PRODUCTION NOTE

The prologues preceding each scene were initially used to cover the scene changes, together with music. In the West End production of the play it was found possible to dispense with the scene prologues, and use suitable interval music only. The prologues preceding Act I and Act II were, however, retained throughout

CHARACTERS

Philip, a freelance journalist
Kathy, a teacher
Len, a crane driver
Tony, a salesman
Douglas, a company director
Nurse (Mary)
Speech Therapist (Ann)
Physiotherapist (Helen)
Kevin, a wheelchair patient (non-speaking; played by an
A.S.M.)

PRE-CURTAIN SEQUENCE

The Lights are lowered, but the Curtain *does not immediately rise*

After a brief pause, the following dialogue comes from loudspeakers

Nurse Can you bath yourself?
Philip Yes, thank you.
Nurse Manage the loo on your own?
Philip Yes.
Nurse Normal diet?
Philip Yes.
Nurse Do you wear dentures?
Philip No.
Nurse Eyesight?
Philip Fine.
Nurse Any need for regular pain killers?
Philip No.
Nurse How about sleep? Do you need drugs?
Philip I've brought some with me.
Nurse You hand those in, collect any drugs you need from the drugs trolley every night. You were warned not to bring much money with you, or any valuables?
Philip Yes.
Nurse Right, Philip, wait outside, and doctor will see you soon. After that you'll be given your programme, and I'll take you along to the gym.

The voices stop

After a brief pause, the Curtain *rises*

ACT I*

The Gymnasium. 9.40 a.m. Monday, Week 1

Sets are described throughout as though they were conventional, but since we are using several different sets, the descriptions are only meant to serve as a basis for the designer

The Gymnasium is just a big room with wall bars. At one end, a square stool on which the Physiotherapist will sit. At the other end, more stools are stacked two or three high. Patients drift in, those in wheelchairs park themselves, those who can walk fetch a stool each, with varying degrees of difficulty

In real life, there would be fifteen to twenty patients or more, rather than just "our" five. Perhaps either use some additional patients, who do not speak, or the scene could be staged so that the audience are persuaded that there are more out of sight

As the CURTAIN *rises, Tony is sitting and doing the* Telegraph *crossword. Tony is a bit either side of forty years of age, a big, well built man, were he not confined to a wheelchair. From the waist up, he is still strong, and "drives" his wheelchair energetically. He seems to be always laughing and cheerful, if not always kind. A pair of elbow crutches are hooked across the back of his wheelchair. He wears a tracksuit and gym shoes. Like all the other patients, he wears a plastic wristband on his left wrist, on which are his name, date of birth and religion*

Douglas makes his way towards the stools. He wears a short sleeved shirt, ordinary trousers and shoes. Douglas is about fifty, a man who always took care of himself, slim build, decisive features. A stroke has affected his left side but, since he is right handed, his speech is unimpaired. As he walks, he holds his affected left hand in front of himself with his good right hand. However, he has perceptual problems due to the loss of the left half of the visual field, and he has to take care not to bump into things on his left side. Douglas's left leg has been fitted with an ortholon splint—made of plastic, moulded to fit under the foot and behind the calf, worn over the sock. Lacking sensation in the affected leg, part of the problem is simply to believe that it will support his weight. Douglas tends to "hop" off the affected leg as fast as possible

The Physiotherapist comes from the entrance to an equipment store (where

---

*N.B. Paragraph 3 on p. ii of this Acting Edition regarding photocopying and video-recording should be carefully read.

the record player is kept) as Douglas is moving across the gymnasium, and speaks as she heads for the corridor

Physiotherapist Put your weight on that left leg, Douglas. It'll support you. Come on.

The Physiotherapist goes into the corridor

Douglas fetches a stool for himself, carrying it in his good right hand, puts it down, sits on it. He begins to lift his affected left arm with his right hand, getting it up as far as he can above his head. It is an exercise he should do automatically and frequently throughout the play

Len enters, wearing shirt, trousers, ordinary shoes. He is in his middle fifties. He walks with something a bit like a sailor's roll, but otherwise there appears to be little wrong with him. Len is a Londoner, the salt of the earth working class type. Decent, amiable, not much formal education, but a fair bit of natural intelligence

Tony Done your number twos, Len? I heard you grunting away in the thunder box.

Len It's not funny mate. I nearly bust a gut, trying.

Tony (*wagging a finger*) No number twos for nurse? Naughty boy. It'll be the enema for you, my lad.

Douglas You do love the sound of your own voice, don't you?

Tony Who said that? Who said that?

Tony looks at Douglas, who is raising his clasped hands

(*Imitating Douglas*) Why, hallelujah.

Len has collected his stool, and sits down on it

The Physiotherapist brings Philip in. At this stage, Philip is wearing shirt, trousers, and ordinary shoes. Philip is in his early to middle forties. He slowly makes his way in using elbow crutches. Were we able to see his legs, both would have suffered considerable muscle wasting, and the left would be markedly thinner than the right. He leans heavily on his elbow crutches. When walking, they are used alternately, as with two walking sticks

Physiotherapist You can change into track suit and gym shoes after this.

Philip Right.

Physiotherapist (*to the others*) This is Philip.

Tony Hallo, again. Saw him arrive.

Physiotherapist He's in your room.

Tony Ah, the new boy.

Physiotherapist (*indicating*) You'll need a stool.

The Physiotherapist goes back into the equipment store

Tony Room Six. Sister reckons she can match people up. Reserved for the bright ones. Well, Len there's not too bright, but he's all right.

Len (*unruffled as ever*) Hallo.

Philip Hallo, Len.

Tony The praying mantis is Douglas. He's not all right.

Douglas How do you do.

Philip Hallo.

Len I'll get a stool for you.

Philip Thanks, but I think I can manage. (*He manoeuvres a stool into position beside Tony, by edging it forward, a few inches at a time, with one of his elbow crutches*)

While Philip is doing this, Tony reverts to his crossword

Tony This should be easy. "Let all detainees go to rehabilitation centre." Two words, four and six. Come on, Len. Let all detainees go to rehabilitation centre—Two words, four and six.

Len Er . . . patients exit.

Tony Four and six, dummy, not eight and four. Patients exit! It's supposed to make sense, you great wally.

Douglas Mass escape.

Tony (*scornfully*) No!

Douglas All right. What is it?

Tony I'm thinking.

Philip Open prison.

Tony Brilliant. (*He writes the answer in*) An acquisition, this lad. Another great brain in Room Six at last.

Len I don't get that.

Tony "Open prison"—let the inmates go. And if this dump isn't a prison, I don't know what is. Besides, it fits with seven down.

Kathy has arrived, and is moving across the gymnasium to fetch a stool. She is in her thirties, wears a loose dress and flat shoes. She would be attractive, except that she moves as though she has lost pride in her own femininity, does not hold herself erect, her movements are rather lax. She has a letter in one hand

Philip has laid his elbow crutches on the floor, and is looking at his programme—a small card. Tony peers at the card

Tony That your programme? What have you got?

Philip Physiotherapy after this, then Gymnasium . . .

Tony (*reading for himself*) And Occupational Therapy *before* and after lunch. Aren't you the lucky one?

Philip I thought there'd be more physiotherapy.

Tony Good God, man, what do you think this is? A rehabilitation centre?

Philip What happens in Occupational Therapy?

Tony Whenever they can't think what to do with us next, they stick down O.T. Keeps us occupied.

Philip (*looking round*) What's it like, this place?

Tony A cross between Butlin's and Belsen. Morning, Kathy.

Kathy is on her way past them with her stool. She pauses, turns her head towards Tony

Kathy Hallo ... uh ... (*She breaks off. The word "Tony" has momentarily eluded her*)

Tony's attitude is wrong. He should allow her time to find the word. He does not. He also speaks as if she were an idiot child

Tony Me Tony, him Philip. Nothing to it. Good morning, Tony. Good morning Philip. Right? Oh, never mind. Read your love letter.

Kathy smiles uncertainly, moves on, sets her stool down some way in front of them, and sits. Tony sighs in Philip's direction, exaggeratedly rotates his right forefinger, indicating, "she's potty"

She's not all there. Car accident. Her boy friend driving, been to a party, thought he was James Hunt. (*He mimes a car rolling over and over*) Addled her brains.

The record player starts playing—off in the equipment room. It is not the best record player in the world, and certainly not hi-fi. The record is Trini Lopez, singing If I had a Hammer (*or similar style and vintage*)

Where they dig up these discs, I'll never know. Buried for posterity somewhere, I should think.

The Physiotherapist comes in, sits on her stool, facing them

She begins to make rhythmic movements, arms, legs, body. As she does so, she speaks, echoing whatever movements she is making; e.g. "Hands on head, shoulders, sideways, back, forward ..." etc.

The Patients follow her movements as best they can, in time to the music, according to their various disabilities

Tony can follow the arm and body movements, but not of course the leg movements

Douglas can use his right arm and right leg, but his left arm remains motionless, and movements of his left leg are hesitant and belated

Len can do it all, but he follows lackadaisically and without interest

Philip, never having done it before, is all at sea. Even when he begins to get the hang of it, and keeps roughly in time with arm and body movements, his legs are not under full control, tend to arrive where they should be late, and he loses the rhythm

Kathy follows the Physiotherapist not only with precision, but with flair, losing herself in the pleasure of doing it

The Physiotherapist stands up

Physiotherapist Those who can, stand up. (*Her movements are now with her legs, as well as arms. One foot sideways—back. The other sideways, back. One leg forward, heel on the floor, back. And so on, all to the beat of the song. Again, she speaks, matching whatever movements she makes; e.g.*

"Right foot sideways, back, left foot sideways, back, forward, back ..." etc.)

Tony, of course, remains in his wheelchair and cannot move his legs. He compromises by following with his hands and arms

Douglas can stand, but he is unhappy about placing weight on his left leg, and, with the weight on his right leg, his left does not answer too well. The overall effect is clumsy and out of time

Kathy is a revelation, suddenly a different woman, graceful and feminine, delighting in the use of her body. Although she remains gyrating on the same spot, she looks as if she is floating and dancing

Philip has groped for his elbow crutches, got them into position, and levered himself to his feet—which all takes time. Leaning on his crutches, he can clumsily imitate some of the leg movements, but when there are arm movements as well, he staggers, nearly losing his balance

Stay seated if you'd rather Philip. (*Not ceasing her movements, speaking above the sound of the music*)

Philip shakes his head and carries on, grimly determined

The effect should be a kind of weird ballet, almost surrealistic—normal life out of sync—both funny and touching. And, with the exception of Kathy, none are too good, all clumsy and uncertain—we need to see a progression in a later Music and Movement session

The Physiotherapist sits down as the record nears its end, and continues with movements sitting down. The Patients follow suit. In Philip's case, by the time he has sat down, placed his crutches on the floor, and got roughly in time with the music again, the record is nearly over

The record comes to an end. The Physiotherapist stands up

Physiotherapist All right, relax, everybody, while I go and change the record.

The Physiotherapist goes into the equipment store to put the next record on

The Patients sit waiting, mostly somewhat apathetically. Tony looks round

Tony (*to Philip*) Like a loony bin, isn't it! A bunch of cripples, trying to wave their hands and feet about.
Philip (*about Kathy*) She seems to enjoy it. . . .
Tony Kathy? She doesn't know any better. Like the Irish turkey looking forward to Christmas.

In front of them Kathy, half sensing that she is being talked about, looks round. Tony smiles and waves at her cheerfully

All right, Pavlova? That's the spirit. Keep it up.

Kathy gives her subdued uncertain smile, faces front again

Another record starts to play. The Floral Dance, *the brass band version with a thump-thump beat but no vocal*

Here we go. Where we all quick march in a soldierly fashion. You'll be all right, Len. You must have done National Service.
Len Good days, they were.

The Physiotherapist comes back in, remains standing

Tony Doug, too, I expect. I'll bet he was an officer, though, by George.
Physiotherapist Stand up, those able.

The Physiotherapist starts with her movements, variations of the previous ones. As before, the Patients follow as best they can

Quite soon, the Physiotherapist's movements come to resemble those of marching on the spot. The Patients' attempts to follow are so ragged as to be pathetic—very different from what we shall finally see

The Lights fade to Black-out

PROLOGUE TO SCENE 2

Dialogue from loudspeakers

Nurse Philip, Sister thinks it would be all right for you to go home for the weekend, if you'd like to.
Philip There may be some mail I should deal with. May as well, I suppose.
Nurse Well, this place can be pretty depressing at weekends. How are you finding it?
Philip It's good to be out of hospital, and doing something positive. But it's a lot more tiring than I'd expected.
Nurse The first week's usually the hardest. Are you settling in with Tony and the others?
Philip Yes, fine.
Nurse Good. Back Sunday then, in time for supper or soon after. Have a good weekend.

SCENE 2

The Speech Therapist's office 2.30 pm. Tuesday. Week 2

An ordinary, quite small office. Bookshelves, two chairs either side of a desk. This could be simply illuminated to one side of the stage

The Speech Therapist wears ordinary clothes, a dress or skirt and blouse. Kathy is sitting facing her

Speech Therapist Remember all the words are connected with transport.

Kathy ... driver ... ticket ... elevator ... platform ... under ... (*She hesitates*) underground ...

Speech Therapist Good.

Kathy ... conductor ... fare ... bus ... destined.

Speech Therapist Are you sure?

Kathy (*looking at the word again*) Destin ... a ... tion.

Speech Therapist Well done. A couple of others weren't quite right. You said "elevator". It's escalator, isn't it?

Kathy Oh yes.

Speech Therapist And it was "bus stop", not "bus". Still that's better. You're making progress. Right. Let's run over some of the exercises we've done. What is your address, Kathy?

Kathy Flat ... (*Pause. She looks tense*) Flat number ... (*Pause*)

Speech Therapist The name of the block?

Kathy Redfearn Court.

Speech Therapist Good. In?

Kathy Atherley Road.

Speech Therapist Fine. Nearly there. Now all we need is the flat number.

Kathy I think ... it's ...

Speech Therapist Don't guess. Is it a single number, or more than one?

Kathy One.

Speech Therapist Well, we know you can count from one to ten quite easily.

Kathy I want to ... know it ... without that.

Speech Therapist You will. Meantime, it's better to get it right.

Kathy One, two, three ... (*A murmur. Subconsciously, she counts on her fingers at the same time*) ... four, five, six, seven, eight ... (*Louder*) Nine. Flat nine.

Speech Therapist (*a smile*) Well done. You're home. Now again. Your address?

Kathy Flat ... (*A brief struggle*) ... nine, Redfearn Court, Atherley Road.

Speech Therapist Right. Good. Until it comes to you at once, and it will in time, don't worry about arriving at the right number by working your way up to it. It only takes a few seconds. Now let's try the really hard one. What is your telephone number, Kathy?

Kathy Oh, dear ... um ... (*Guessing madly*) Two, eight, three ... no ... Oh two three ... no, that can't be ...

Speech Therapist Why can't it?

Kathy Oh first ... is ... a long ... way ...

Speech Therapist That's right. A trunk call Good. Have one more try. Is the first number a high one? (*She writes Kathy's telephone number down on a piece of paper*)

Kathy No ... small ... not one ...

Speech Therapist Right. Not one.

Kathy Two? ... no ... three ... three? ... is it three? ...

Speech Therapist Yes. So it's three ... ?

Kathy Three ... (*A murmur*) One, two three ... two?

Speech Therapist Good.

Kathy Three ... two ... (*Pause. A determined rush*) Three, two, eight, oh, seven, nine, four.

Speech Therapist (*amused*) Well, that's certainly a brave try. (*She passes a slip of paper to Kathy*) This is your number. Read it aloud.

Kathy (*reading*) Three ... two ... oh ... two ... eight ... seven ... three ... (*Disappointed*) It is ... nothing like ...

Speech Therapist Numbers are a problem, Kathy. We know you can now say the days of the week and the months of the year from memory, but the sequence in a telephone number—there's no rhyme or reason to it. On the other hand, until you *can* memorize your phone number, it doesn't matter. At home, it's on your telephone, if anyone wants it. Let's do something more concrete. Where you can see the problem. Handling money. (*She takes some money from her handbag*) Suppose you've been shopping, and it comes to one pound, forty five pence. I'd like you to give me the exact amount.

Kathy First, can I say the ... (*she forgets "alphabet"*) the A B C?

Speech Therapist Kathy, I have explained, being able to memorize your A B C doesn't matter. The alphabet isn't used in communication.

Kathy Alphabet, yes. Say it.

Speech Therapist Kathy, even if you can, you don't go around saying the alphabet to other people.

Kathy Please. Let me.

Speech Therapist Well, all right. If it's important to you, it's important. But try taking the letters in small groups.

Kathy takes a breath. This self-imposed hurdle is vitally important to her

Kathy A ... B ... C ... (*Pause*) ... D ... E ... H ...
Speech Therapist D, E, F.
Kathy F ... D ... E ... F ... (*Pause*) ... H ... K ...
Speech Therapist G, H, I.
Kathy (*getting distressed*) G ... K ... M ...
Speech Therapist Let's leave it, Kathy. Don't worry about it. It is very difficult.

Kathy is on the verge of frustrated tears

Kathy It won't come ...
Speech Therapist There's a reason. Let me tell you. All right?

Kathy regains control. She nods

We need language to communicate, to express thoughts and ideas. But because of your accident, your retrieval mechanism is faulty. You sometimes lose access to the language store—but you haven't lost the language store itself. That's still there, in your mind.

Kathy I know. I know it's there. But I can't ... I can't find ... find things. Names of things. I know what they are, but ... what they're called ... it won't come out.

Speech Therapist Exactly, and that's what we're working on. That's the point of all these exercises, and you've improved a lot, you know.

Kathy Some things. But . . . lots of things, not. Simple things. Like the A B
. . . alphabet. (*Softly, as if drumming it into her head*) Alphabet.

Speech Therapist The alphabet isn't simple, Kathy. There are only seven
days in the week. One to ten, ten numbers; twelve months in the year. But
the alphabet has twenty six letters, and that's too many factors at this
stage. It's not easy, and honestly it's not something you should worry
about.

Kathy It is important. One of the first things I learned . . . now I can't say it
. . . I want to . . .

Speech Therapist The trouble is . . . (*A quick glance at her watch*) . . . there's
only so much time. Suppose I put it on a cassette, so that you can listen to
it in your own time?

Kathy (*happy*) Oh, yes, please.

Speech Therapist Play it over and over, and try and see the letters in your
mind.

Kathy (*studying money on desk*) The . . . what you said I bought . . .

Speech Therapist Shopping.

Kathy Shopping. How much?

Speech Therapist We'd better leave that until tomorrow, now. Time's
running out.

Kathy Could I . . . (*pointing at book*) . . . that . . . the . . . um . . .

Speech Therapist Poem?

Kathy Yes . . . the one . . . by . . . (*She cannot remember*)

Speech Therapist Robert Herrick?

Kathy Yes . . . read . . . again . . .

Speech Therapist It might be better to keep to simpler things for a while.
You did find it very difficult last time, Kathy.

Kathy Try . . . please . . . I could . . . once . . .

Speech Therapist Why is that particular poem so special?

Kathy At school . . . when I was . . . small . . . one Parents' Day . . . I had to
. . . say it . . . no book . . . there's a word . . .

Speech Therapist Recite it.

Kathy Recite it, yes.

Speech Therapist Well, since you once knew it by heart, that could help.
Let's look at it again in a week or two.

Kathy Now . . . please . . .

Speech Therapist It'll take us a long time to work our way through it, and I
think Andrew's waiting outside.

Kathy Not hard . . . words . . . I was . . . small . . . could then . . . words
short . . .

Speech Therapist Yes, but the concepts are difficult, you found that before.
(*Glancing at poem in book*) Suppose I mark it for you, where you might
have problems. Then you can look at it on your own, before we have
another shot at it. All right?

Kathy Yes.

Speech Therapist Fine. We'll do that. See you tomorrow, Kathy.

The Lights fade to Black-out

PROLOGUE TO SCENE 3

Dialogue from loudspeakers

Philip is having a bath. Sound of water splashing, and a door being rattled hard—and then again

Philip Yes? Who is it?

Douglas Will you be long, Philip?

Philip Just got in. The shower's free.

Douglas It's not. Len's in there. Besides, I don't like showers. I prefer a bath.

Philip Give me five minutes.

Douglas I always make a point of bathing immediately after tea. I thought that was understood.

Philip Douglas you can't reserve the bloody bathroom. Today I got here first for once, all right?

Douglas (*after a pause*) I'll just hang on outside, if you don't mind. If I turn my back, someone else'll get in before me.

SCENE 3

Room Six. 5.30 pm. Wednesday. Week 3

A ward for four men. Four hospital beds, four bedside lockers, four smallish wardrobes. But only one wash-basin, with a large mirror, above which is a notice, NO SMOKING. *The electric razor plug is set low—so that it can be used by patients in wheelchairs. The door is propped open. Outside, a corridor at right angles*

Douglas's bed is on the right hand side. Len has the equivalent one on the left hand side. The other two are Philip's and Tony's, Philip's on the right hand side, Tony's on the left

It is late afternoon. Treatment for the day is over. Philip and Douglas have bathed, and are changing for the evening

Philip has shirt and trousers on, and is sitting on his bed, putting his shoes on. After that, he waits until Douglas has finished—their wardrobes adjoin and there is not much space between Douglas's bed and the wardrobes

Douglas has his trousers on, and a vest. He takes a shirt from a hanger in the wardrobe, puts it on, coat style, and buttons it, using his right hand. He is pretty adept at this by now

During this, Philip has eased his shoes on, bending forward, using his body weight to slip them on, and then picks up the Patients' Handbook *from his locker and begins to study it*

Douglas You must know that off by heart.

Philip Pretty well.

Douglas (*quoting*) "All patients should bring any appliances they normally use, such as crutches, supports, leg braces, wheelchairs . . ."

Philip Sounds familiar. Another student of the *Patients' Handbook*.

Douglas Read it once. I have that kind of memory.

Philip "Appliances patients normally use." What's normal about appliances?

Douglas Ghastly word.

Philip Why not "aids which patients temporarily need"? Something more positive.

Douglas (*quoting again*) "Daily Timetable. Seven fifteen a.m. Early morning call. Male patients are expected to shave before breakfast." That's positive enough.

Philip One or two of the female patients as well.

During the above, Douglas has crossed to Philip, and holds out his right arm

Douglas Would you mind?

Philip buttons Douglas's right sleeve

Meantime, out in the corridor, we hear the sound of Kathy's cassette recorder as she approaches. The Speech Therapist's voice saying the alphabet, slowly and deliberately, A. . . . B. . . . C. . . . etc.

Kathy pauses at the doorway, the cassette recorder in one hand and a cellophane wrapped bunch of flowers in the other, and glances in through the open door. She sees Douglas, and moves out of sight to her own room, the cassette recording of the alphabet receding, until it is unheard

Neither Philip nor Douglas take any notice — they have become used to it, part of the scenery

Douglas God, I never expected to find myself anywhere like this.

Philip (*drily*) No. Serious illness is something which happens to other people.

Douglas Me? Have a stroke? Never crossed my mind. Always looked after myself, played squash two or three times a week. Why me?

Philip Why any of us? It doesn't much matter. We're all here.

Douglas Damned hard to come to terms with, though. You must feel the same.

Philip I suppose I've turned inwards. I can only think of getting better. Being able to walk without "appliances", play tennis again, there's no room for anything else.

Douglas Some have settled already, you know. Given up. Accepted it. (*About his arm*) I'll get this blasted thing working again if it kills me. (*He moves to his wardrobe*) This leg too. I need to get back to the office as soon as possible. (*He reaches into his wardrobe, takes his jacket from a hanger, slips it on, using his right hand in a practised way, locks his wardrobe door, pockets the key*)

Philip Don't you run your own company?

Douglas I'm one of the directors. I don't own it.

Philip Well, your speech hasn't been affected.

Douglas That's not the point. I'd just taken delivery of a new Mercedes.

Philip On the company?

Douglas Naturally.

Philip They can give you a chauffeur.

Douglas I don't want a chauffeur. I intend to drive my own car, thank you. I refuse to ask for special treatment. I refuse to be disabled. Simple as that.

Douglas goes, though his left side brushes the door as he leaves, and we hear the slightly uneven sound of his receding footsteps

Philip takes a small bottle of whisky from under his pillow, and swallows a mouthful. There is a tap on the door

It is Kathy, who is holding a notebook. The propped open door shields her from Philip's line of vision. Philip puts the bottle back under his pillow

Philip Come in.

Kathy enters hesitantly, although with inner determination

Hallo, Kathy.

Kathy Excuse me ...

Philip It's all right. Come on in.

Kathy has geared herself up for this and the most important word comes out first

Kathy Writer.

Philip (*taken aback*) Sorry?

Kathy Writer ... (*Pointing at door*) ... they say ... (*Pointing at Philip*) ... you ...

Philip Oh, I see. Well, I'm a journalist.

Kathy But you write ... things ...

Philip Yes. Features, mostly.

Kathy Please ... teach me ... will you? (*She offers her notebook*)

Philip To write?

Kathy Yes.

Philip Well ... what do you have in mind? Articles? Reports for your local paper or something?

Kathy No ... if you ... write ...

Philip Yes? Go on.

Kathy You must know ... how ... (*Miming handwriting*)

Philip Oh. Yes. Well, I generally use a typewriter.

Kathy But ... you can.

Philip I can. Yes.

Kathy I could. Not now ... only print ... not proper writing ... joined up ...

Philip Handwriting?

Kathy Yes. Will you show me, please?

Philip We'd better sit down. (*He makes his way to his bed, sits down, parks his elbow crutches*)

Kathy sits beside Philip and he takes the pad

Kathy Thank you ... (*She twists his plastic wristband to see his name*) ... Philip ... I did know ... but it went ...

Philip My handwriting's pretty awful. Still ... What would you like?

Kathy Anything. That. (*She points to the* Patients' Handbook)

Philip (*reading it*) Oh, the *Patients' Handbook*. "Getting well is a full time occupation for you, so treatment goes on. ..."

Kathy (*shaking her head*) No. One ... a few words, and then ... more.

Philip One phrase at a time.

Kathy Yes. I forgot my pen.

Philip That's all right (*He produces a pen*)

Philip writes slowly and carefully. Kathy watches the movements of his fingers and pen intently

Kathy (*As he writes*) Getting ... Well ... is ...

Philip Well, at least you can read it.

Kathy I can read! (*She snatches the handbook and begins to read from it painfully*) "... special treatment ... re ..." (*She breaks off*)

Philip Required.

Kathy Let me.

Philip Sorry.

Kathy "... special treatment ... required ... to speed ... recovery ..." (*Looking at Philip*) More?

Philip If you like.

Kathy "... only by your ... own ... efforts ... can you ... get better; we will show you ... how ... to do it ..." (*She returns the handbook to Philip*) I can ... it is hard ... the words ... but I can ...

Philip That's good. But what I meant was, you can read my handwriting.

Kathy Yes. "Getting well is ..."

Philip Right. Well, you copy it underneath.

Kathy takes the pad and pen, studies the pad dubiously, and looks at Philip

Kathy First ... if I ... big letters ... (*She mimes the act of printing letters*)

Philip Print. Fine. You do it your way first. (*Pointing*) Down here.

Kathy That's a nice pen. (*She carefully prints the phrase*)

Philip Getting ... well ... is ... OK. Now copy what I've written in your own hand. On the line underneath.

Kathy seems to need to steel herself for this task. She bends her head, childlike, over the page, concentrating fiercely. But the pen scarcely moves. For a long moment, she appears to be frozen. Finally

Kathy I can't ...

To Philip's horror, he perceives that Kathy is unreasonably distressed, and weeping

Philip Kathy, come on ... try again ... there's nothing to cry about ...

Philip attempts to place a consoling hand on her arm. Kathy openly sobbing now, hurries blindly towards the door

Kathy, wait. (*He grabs for his elbow crutches, and attempts to stand up in order to follow her. It is a reflex action, but Philip's physical condition is not geared to sudden movements. He loses his balance, and falls awkwardly on to the floor with a crash, losing his grip on his elbow crutches, which go clattering and flying*)

The noise brings Kathy to a stop. She sees what has happened

Kathy Oh! (*She hurries back to Philip*) Philip ... you all right?
Philip (*shaken*) Don't know ... (*Lying on his face, he pushes with his hands, trying to turn over*)
Kathy Let me ...
Philip If I could just sit up.

Kathy, nothing wrong with her body, straightens his legs

Sorry.
Kathy Come ... against the bed ... (*Suiting action to words, she slides Philip round until he is leaning against the bed*)

Philip gets one elbow up on to the bed, attempts to lift himself and fails

Philip Oh, hell.
Kathy Just ... arms ... here ... (*Putting Philip's arms round her*)
Philip Careful. You'll hurt yourself. You'd better ring for the nurse.
Kathy It's all right ... this way ... there ...

And Philip is back on his bed sprawling, somewhat breathless. With Philip's arms levering on the bed, and hers under his legs, Kathy has been able to lift him up. She retrieves his elbow crutches, hands them to him, and stands beside him

Philip (*as she does so*) You're stronger than you look.
Kathy Are you all right? (*Her distress has gone*)
Philip I think so. (*He prods his legs experimentally*) One thing about not much sensation in the legs, it doesn't hurt if you knock yourself. I really am sorry, Kathy.
Kathy Not you. Me. My fault.
Philip It's so bloody humiliating.
Kathy Please? I didn't ... you speak fast ...
Philip (*more slowly*) I said it was very humiliating.
Kathy What?
Philip Falling down. Needing help to get up again.
Kathy You can speak ... you can write. For me, it is ... what you said ...
Philip Humiliating.

Kathy To know something here (*her head*), and it will not come out here (*her mouth*) ... that is ... (*an effort*) ... humiliating.

Philip I wasn't laughing at you.

Kathy I know. It was ... it is hard ... the words ...

Philip Take your time. There's no hurry. Tell me.

Kathy Sometimes, I cry ... no reason ... I know it's not ... sensible ... I can't stop. Sometimes, I laugh ... no reason ... I know what I'm doing ... but I can't help it. Crying like that ... laughing like that ... I know how ... (*Gesturing*) ... other people look at me. What they think.

Philip But you know you're aware. You're still yourself. OK, part of you doesn't function as it used to, that's why you're here, to put that right. There are times when I feel much the same. In my case, my legs don't work properly.

Kathy With you ... what matters ... hasn't changed ...

Philip Outside in the real world, with these (*his crutches*), people on the street look at me and then they look away. (*He smiles at Kathy*) At least you can walk along the street, and no one will look at you like that.

Kathy If I had crutches ... or a wheelchair like... Tony ... instead of this ... I could still work.

Philip What did you do?

Kathy I was a teacher in ... a school for ... small children.

Philip A nursery school?

Kathy No. The next ...

Philip A primary school.

Kathy Yes ... I was a teacher in a primary school.

Philip My father wanted me to go in for teaching, but I didn't like the idea.

Kathy I love it ... the little ones ... teaching. But if I can't say to them ... not say ... another word ... cuh something ...

Philip Communicate?

Kathy Yes, if I can't ... find the words when they ask ... not about the lesson, but ... other questions ... a kind I am not ready for ...

Philip Unexpected?

Kathy Unexpected questions ... children are not patient ... if I cannot find the words ... cannot write (*miming*) on the blackboard. ...

Philip Is the alphabet to do with this as well?

Kathy Yes.

Philip Well, if you ever want to try it on me ...

Kathy Really?

Philip Any time.

Kathy Now?

Philip (*taken aback*) Er ... yes ... fine.

Kathy Are you sure?

Philip Yes. Whenever you're ready.

Kathy Well ... A ... B ... C ... D ... E ... (*Pause*)

Philip Do you want me to prompt you?

Kathy No. I've been listening to the ... thing ... a lot. D ... E ... F ... (*Beginning to rush—a touch of panic*) ... J ... Q ... P ... Q ...

Philip No, no, there's only one Q, and it comes towards the end.

Kathy slaps her leg, or her hands together—some gesture of frustration

Leave it. We'll try again tomorrow. You got the first six letters right. That's a start.

Kathy But I want to say all.

Philip You will, Kathy. It'll come. It'll all come.

Kathy (*grateful*) You seem so sure.

Philip (*about his elbow crutches*) As sure as I'm going to throw these away, and dash all over the world again.

Kathy The world . . . where?

Philip Anywhere someone wants me to go.

Kathy Very . . . exciting.

Philip It's a living. No, I enjoy it. Can't wait to get back to it. Sometimes, just now and then, you get lucky, and you're in the right place at the right time, and you meet the right people, and then you find the right words, and you know what you've written is true and good, and that makes all the rest worthwhile.

Kathy Someone I know . . . travels . . . very much . . .

Philip The friend who was driving?

Kathy Yes. Sam.

Philip Was he hurt?

Kathy No.

Philip Do you remember it? The accident?

Kathy No.

Philip Does he come and see you?

Kathy looks at Philip

Sam.

Kathy He works for an . . . oil company. He is often . . . away.

Philip Still, you get flowers, and letters.

Kathy Yes. Do you have . . . people who come to see you?

Philip Visitors? (*A negative*) Those I'd like to see, I'd rather not see them here. That can wait. I just want to concentrate on getting better. You may not feel the same way . . .

Kathy I do. This is . . . for us . . . now . . . not . . . (*She gives up trying to express the thought*)

Philip If your car breaks down, you leave the thing in the garage until it's fixed. Let's get ourselves repaired first.

Kathy smiles

Without warning, since a wheelchair doesn't make much noise, Tony comes swinging into the room, speaking on the move as he sees them

Tony Hallo, hallo, what's all this? Girls in the dorm? Nooky in Room Six? Kathy. What *would* your boyfriend say? (*He continues across to his locker from which he takes a packet of cigarettes*)

Kathy, startled, stands up at once

Just kidding, love. Shan't say a word. Forgot my fags, that's all.

Kathy hurries out, distressed

Philip gathers together his elbow crutches, and stands up

Oh, gawd, she's off again.

Philip Tony, there are occasions when I feel like shoving one of these crutches up your nostrils, and this is one of them.

Tony You raise your crutch to me, sir, and by heaven I'll run you over with my wheelchair.

Philip For Christ's sake stop treating the girl as if she were an idiot. She's not. Her self-respect's damaged, she's easily hurt, and in future you show some understanding. Bloody remember that. (*He stomps forward towards the door with such dignity as is possible, when using elbow crutches*)

Tony Come on, Phil. I didn't mean anything . . .

But Philip has gone

Well, can't have tantrums in the dorm as well as hanky panky. (*He wheels himself towards the door, calling as he goes*) Philip, Kathy. Tony's sorry. Tony begs forgiveness on bended knees. Well, no, can't quite manage that. Kathy. Philip . . .

The Lights fade to Black-out

PROLOGUE TO SCENE 4

Dialogue from loudspeakers

Philip is exercising in Room Six in his free time, during the evening

Nurse Oh, you're here, Philip.

Philip Hallo, Mary. Want me?

Nurse Telephone message. Peter called. Make sense?

Philip Yes. A friend. I'll call him back tomorrow.

Nurse What were you doing when I came in?

Philip I asked them in physio to give me some exercises I could do in my own time. I'd rather work on those for an hour than sit and watch television. I thought I'd be better than this by now.

Nurse You expected rather a lot in three weeks.

Philip I do expect a lot, Mary.

Nurse Well, I'll leave you to it. Good night.

Philip (*resuming exercises*) Good night, Mary.

Scene 4

Physiotherapy. 10.00 a.m. Thursday. Week 3

The equipment in use is not complicated: a few of the ubiquitous square stools; a mat on the floor for floor work; practise stairs, three or four steps up, three or

*four steps down the other side, with a handrail on both sides; a plinth; a
medicine ball; a couple of footballs*

*Philip and Tony are wearing tracksuits. (We do not want to see that the
actors' legs are not in fact wasted) Both have bare feet*

*Douglas is wearing gym shorts, and a tennis shirt. His feet are also bare, that
is, he is not wearing his ortholon splint. The splint is always worn with normal
shoes, and over the sock. Without his splint, Douglas will have some degree of
foot drop—the toes of the left foot tend to scrape the floor as he walks. He
could easily trip if he is not careful. He is practising going up and down the
stairs by himself, holding the banister with his right hand*

Tony is sitting in his wheelchair

*Philip is kneeling on the mat. The Physiotherapist is kneeling in front of him
and pushing his pelvis in different directions*

Physiotherapist Hold ... hold ... don't let me push you ... hold ... hold
... keep that position ... hold it ... hold it ... you're not trying hard
enough.
Philip I'm doing my best.
Physiotherapist Hold ... hold ... you're not concentrating ... (*Still pushing
Philip*) Hold ... hold ... Douglas, you don't need to heave yourself up
like that. Your left leg's quite capable of lifting you. (*To Philip*) Hold it ...
put a bit more effort into it ... hold ... hold ... that's better ... that's
much better ... Good. All right, relax for a minute.

Philip "relaxes" by going forward on to his hands, all fours style

The Physiotherapist gets up

Physiotherapist Douglas, on the stool, please. Right, Tony.

Douglas leaves the stairs and sits on a stool

The Physiotherapist hands a medicine ball to Tony

You two carry on.
Tony (*to Philip*) Ready?
Philip No! Hang on. (*He regains a kneeling position by moving his hands
backwards, and then up to his knees*)

OK.

*Tony throws the medicine ball at his chest. Philip catches it in his kneeling
position, throws it back to Tony, who returns it ... and so on. While this is
going on, the Physiotherapist crosses to Douglas, who knows what comes next!
and has already linked his left and right hands*

Physiotherapist Let's straighten things up a bit first. (*She takes Douglas's
left arm and straightens it. Then she straightens his fingertips for him*)

Philip receives the ball from Tony nearly falling off balance

Philip Bloody hell. (*He throws the ball back at Tony*)
Physiotherapist He's not a skittle, Tony. No need to try and knock him flat.
(*To Douglas*) That's better. Now you can clasp your hands properly.

Douglas does so

Fine. Off you go.

*Douglas begins to lift his hands as high as he can aiming to get above his head.
The Physiotherapist watches him for a few moments*

The left arm as high as you can. I think it'll go up a bit more. (*She lightly
takes Douglas's left wrist, "feeling" his movements, guiding it a fraction
higher*)

That's it. That's better. Right, carry on in your own time. (*Turning away*)
Philip, rest for a minute, and then over to the wall bars. Tony, over to the
plinth.

*Philip crawls to the wall bars, beside which are his elbow crutches, and heaves
himself into a sitting position*

Tony wheels himself to the plinth

Douglas doggedly continues with his hands above head exercise

Tony Right ma'am. Worth waiting for. Ready when you are.

*Tony holds out his arms as the Physiotherapist crosses to him. She is trained to
use her back, and can lift heavy men with surprising ease. Tony's arms go
round her, hers go round him*

Oh, this is very intimate. Oh, I like it.
Physiotherapist Hold on tighter.
Tony Have a care, woman. You go too far.

*And with a seemingly effortless lift, Tony is sitting on the edge of the end of the
plinth*

Reminds me of an Australian man's idea of foreplay. "Brace yourself,
Sheil."

Philip, having got his breath has now got to his feet with his elbow crutches

Physiotherapist (*to Tony*) Just stay there for a minute.
Tony Helen, don't be daft. Where the hell do you think I'm going?

The Physiotherapist is watching Philip

Physiotherapist Philip. Just a minute.

Philip pauses, close to the wall bars. The Physiotherapist comes close to him

Give me those. We don't really approve of them, here. (*She takes Philip's
elbow crutches away and props them up against the wall bars*)

Philip extends one hand to support himself on the wall bars

I want you to stand without them. (*She places her fingertips at the sides of Philip's shoulders*)

Hand off the bars.

Philip reluctantly releases the bars, and wobbles a bit

I shan't let you fall. Have you got your balance?
Philip More or less.
Physiotherapist Do you feel safe?
Philip Not especially, no.
Physiotherapist Let yourself rely on your legs.
Philip (*wobbling a bit*) Easier said than done.
Physiotherapist Feel that you've got your weight on both legs. Feel it. I know the left one's weaker, but get your weight on both equally. That's it. That's better. Now, I'm going to move back a bit, and you put your fingers on mine. (*She takes a small backward step, and extends her arms, palms upwards, fingers straight*)

Philip hurriedly rests his hands on hers

Physiotherapist Not on my hands. I don't want you to lean on me. Just my fingertips, so that you're taking your own weight.

Philip cautiously moves his fingers into the desired position

Philip There?
Physiotherapist That's it. Get your balance again. Weight on both legs. Both. Good. Now, bring your right leg forward.

After a "double take" at his right leg, Philip uncertainly does so, and the Physiotherapist moves back slightly to accommodate him

Put your weight on that leg. Now bring the other leg forward.

Philip does so

Douglas has ceased his exercise to watch as well

Physiotherapist Rock from side to side and ... forward again ... rock ... forward ... rock ... forward ... again ... rock ... again.

They have crept a few paces towards a stool, of which the Physiotherapist is aware

Good. (*Expertly, she hooks one foot round the stool, and moves it into position behind Philip*)

Sit down, and relax.

Philip gropes for the stool, and lowers himself onto it

Philip That was hard work. (*Looking at the short distance traversed*) All that way.
Physiotherapist I think you could manage on two sticks, now.
Philip (*pleasantly surprised*) Really?

The Physiotherapist fetches elbow crutches and hands them to him

Physiotherapist Do you feel ready?
Philip To get rid of these? I can't wait.
Physiotherapist All right. We'll fix you up at the end of the session. Have a
breather, and then practise the balance exercises over at the wall bars.

*Tony has been watching all this with mixed feelings. Glad that Philip has
accomplished his stride forward, he would be more than human if he did not
feel envy as well*

Right, Tony. Your turn now.
Tony Oh, goody. I thought you were going to work on your star pupil there
all day.

Douglas resumes his hands over head exercise

Physiotherapist (*to Tony*) Lie back.
Tony And think of England, I know. (*He lies back on the plinth. His legs are
dangling over the edge*)

*The Physiotherapist places one hand on the instep of one of his legs, and the
other hand on his thigh towards the knee of the same leg. Before starting, she
glances at Douglas*

Oh, that's delicious. You wouldn't care to go a bit higher up, I suppose?
Physiotherapist Douglas, that's enough of that one. Practise some walking
now.

*Douglas unclasps his hands which are in the "down" position. When he stands
up, he forgets to hold his left arm forward, and "leaves it behind"*

(*Still holding Tony*) Don't leave that left hand behind when you stand up.
Douglas Sorry. Forgot. (*He "picks up" his left hand*)
Physiotherapist I know, but try not to, otherwise you could easily knock
yourself without realising.
Tony Helen, have a heart and get started, will you? You're driving me mad.
(*But he is lifting his head to look at the Physiotherapist's hand on the inside
of his thigh. He cannot actually feel it in the way he likes to make out*)
Physiotherapist (*to Douglas*) Make sure you're putting your weight on that
left leg. I don't want to see you hopping off it. Getting the "feel" of the
movement, that's the important thing.

Douglas walks across the gym, turns, goes back to his starting point, and so on

*Philip gets up from his stool, moves to the wall bars, parks his elbow crutches
against the bars and, using his hands for support as lightly as possible, begins
balance exercises*

We've done this one before, Tony.
Tony I know. Where you shout at me.
Physiotherapist That's it. I'm going to pull your leg, and on the command
pull, you lift up hard ... now ... PULL! ... and turn ... and PUSH
DOWN! ...

The Physiotherapist's commands are really barked; the sharp tone designed to induce as much effort from the patient as possible. The movements of Tony's legs are, as it were north east to south west, and—the later reverse—north west to south east

    ... and PULL! ... and turn ... and PUSH DOWN! ... that was really feeble, try harder.

Tony I am trying.

Physiotherapist You can do better than that. Come on. And PULL! ... and turn ... and PUSH DOWN! ... and PULL! ... and PUSH DOWN! ...

The Lights fade to Black-out

PROLOGUE TO SCENE 5

Dialogue from loudspeakers

Room Six

Tony What do you scribble all the time in that notebook of yours?

Philip Shorthand.

Tony I deduced that, mate, when I had a shufti one day, and couldn't read it. You keeping a diary or something?

Philip More of a record, a journal.

Tony About what?

Philip This place. What happens.

Tony What for? Sod all happens here.

Philip I don't know. Writing's a habit, I suppose. Something to do. Can I give you a hand?

Tony No, thanks. Safely in bed. Amazing how you can cope when you ... oh, shit.

Philip What?

Tony Hand me my dirty magazine, will you? Ta. That's better. You get on with your gripping account of Occupational Therapy, old son. Me, I'll remind myself of the delights to come this weekend.

SCENE 5

The Patients' Lounge. 9.00 pm. Thursday. Week 4

Rows of somewhat dilapidated easy chairs with wooden arms ranged around the walls, a few tables about the size of card tables here and there, some large floor standing ashtrays

Douglas and Len are playing draughts

Parked to one side, hunched in a wheelchair, is a motionless figure (Kevin) his back to the audience, lit perhaps so that he is a silhouette. No one takes any notice of him

The adjoining room is the TV room. The sound of a suitable programme, half heard, perhaps one of those comedy or variety shows with lots of idiotic laughter and applause

It is the late stages of the game. Douglas concentrating fiercely, Len impassive and casual. Two or three moves are played in silence

Philip is idly watching. Tony is looking at his crossword without enthusiasm. They have finished their evening hot drinks and there is nothing to do until bedtime

Douglas I think we may as well call it a draw, Len.

Philip (*to Douglas*) What? He can win in two moves.

Douglas (*dignified*) I was setting a trap for him. He'd have moved there ... (*Moving a piece*) ...

Len Saw that coming a mile off, mate. (*He picks up a paperback, and starts to read*)

Douglas stares at Len bleakly

Tony Well, how shall we round off another perfect day? Hang gliding? Aerobics? Ballroom dancing?

Tony looks at their faces but gets no response

Kathy walks in, carrying a plastic cup and her cassette recorder, which is quietly playing the alphabet. She sits well away from them on her own. She listens intently to the recording

Squash? Tennis? Charades? Oh, Kathy, give it a rest, will you.

Philip pokes Tony with one of his sticks

Philip Watch it, you.

Kathy looks across enquiringly

Kathy Sorry?

Tony Fancy a game of Scrabble, dear?

Kathy smiles, shakes her head goes back to her recording. She also has the poetry book with her

Tony opens his Telegraph. *He looks at his watch*

There's a film on BBC2, *The Living Dead*. Shan't bother. Couldn't tell the difference. (*He folds the paper, and studies the crossword*)

Len turns a page of his paperback, engrossed. Douglas contemplates the middle distance. Finally:

Douglas I finished my rocking horse, today.

Philip Oh, yes.

Douglas The girl in Occupational Therapy ... oh ... she's in charge of the Heavy Workshop, dark rather bossy ...

Tony (*without looking up*) Hitler.

Douglas Helga. She thought it was very good. To say it was all done with one hand, I was quite pleased, I must say.

Pause

Philip (*politely*) What will you start on next?
Douglas It still has to be painted.
Philip Oh.
Douglas Sandpapered, undercoat, top coat. (*Pause*) Several undercoats. I like to do a job properly. Even if it's only making a rocking horse.
Tony Mine looks more like a decrepit rat. (*Pause*) Here's one for you, Len. Len.
Len (*looking up*) What?
Tony (*as for a crossword clue*) Who rode a camel backwards across the Sahara Desert?
Len (*frowning*) Is it one of them anagrams?
Tony No, it's Lawrence of Dublin.
Douglas Do you only know Irish jokes?
Tony Like the Irish mosquito who caught malaria? Or the Irish woodworm, found dead in a brick? More? No? Oh, well . . . (*He goes back to his crossword*)
Len I remember a joke, I heard once.
Tony (*looking up*) Really?
Len Don't know why. I always forget them. Made me smile, though.
Tony This must be a cracker. I'll write it down.
Len Donkeys' years ago now.
Tony Is that how it begins?
Len No, I'm explaining. This happens during the war, or perhaps it was before . . . or just after . . .
Tony Len, never mind the historical perspective. Just get on with it.
Len Well, there was this little boy, didn't know what to do with himself, getting on his mother's nerves, and he said "Mum, I want to go to the pictures," and she said, "There's pictures on the wall," and he said, "They don't move," and she said, "I'll make the buggers move." (*He mimes an angry gesture of someone swinging a picture*)
Tony Is that it?
Len See in those days, there was no telly, just the radio, wireless it was called then, there wasn't much on that either . . .
Tony Yes, we grasped the point, thank you, Len. You conjured up the picture for us. Picture! How old was this little boy? About ten?
Len (*unruffled*) Could be, I suppose.
Tony Must be the same one, went into a pub one day clutching a handful of silver, reached up, rapped on the counter, and said, "A pint of bitter, please." The landlord looked down at him, and said, "I can't serve you," and the little boy said, "Well fetch some bugger who can." (*He goes back to his crossword for a few moments, and then hands the paper to Philip*) Here. Left an easy one for you.
Len (*chuckling—getting the point*) Fetch some bugger who can. (*He is patting the inside of his left knee anxiously*)

Tony Thinking of leaving us, Len?
Len Reckon I'd better. (*He stands up*)
Tony You're obsessed with that bag. It's a neurosis.
Len If the bag gets over-full the bloody thing leaks all down my leg. Horrible. Can't stand it.

Len goes

Philip (*answer to crossword*) Prick. (*He returns the* Telegraph *and pen to Tony*)
Tony Eh?
Philip Needle result—prick.
Tony Oh, yes. Very good. I knew it was, of course. Doesn't it make you sick?

Pause

Tony Len's started seeing the head shrinker.
Philip Why?
Tony Depression. You know, pills and friendly chats telling him to look on the bright side. Still, I suppose it'll get him out of OT now and then, and gymnasium, all those games with bean bags and hoops and footballs . . .
Douglas Reminds me of being at kindergarten.
Tony I think they're only keeping Len here while they try and work out what to do with him.

The Nurse walks in at this point. She wears a white uniform with a belt but no cap, and is carrying a cellophane-wrapped bunch of flowers—nice, but not too huge

Nurse (*as she enters*) Oh, there you are, Kathy. Flowers for you.

Kathy switches off her cassette recorder. The Nurse hands the flowers to her

They came this afternoon, but they went next door by mistake. The porter's just brought them over.

Kathy takes the flowers

Tony He still loves you, darling.

The Nurse crosses to the immobile, hunched figure in the wheelchair, and wheels him out, speaking as she goes

Nurse Time to start getting you ready for bed, Kevin. You've had your hot drink, haven't you? Your mother's coming to see you at the weekend, as usual. You'll like that, won't you? Something to look forward to. Not long now . . .

If Kevin hears any of this, he gives no indication of having done so

Tony (*to Philip*) Have you seen his mother?
Philip No.

Kathy gets up and goes, taking her flowers with her

Tony Kevin's eighteen. Motor bike accident. She must be about thirty seven, thirty eight.

Douglas Looks younger.

Tony Slim, nice legs, curves where they count, a real little cracker.

Douglas She's always got a smile for him, feeds him, completely matter of fact, chats away to him, as though he understood every word.

Tony I think she fancies me.

Douglas Oh, yes. You and ... who was it? ... Ironside?

Tony A man can detect those subtle signals, Douglas. I expect you've forgotten what it's like.

Douglas I certainly don't indulge in sexual fantasies whenever a young woman gives me a polite smile, if that's what you mean.

Tony Oh, Douglas strikes back. Much longer here, and we'll turn you into a human being yet. (*Thoughtfully*) Poor cow, she probably cries all the way home.

Douglas looks at his watch, places his left arm across his chest, and stands up

Douglas I think I shall go and clean my teeth in peace before you two monopolize the wash-basin.

Tony It's all right, old chap. Just put them in to soak. We don't mind.

Douglas makes his slightly uneven way out

One more fag, and then bye-byes. (*He lights a cigarette*) Saw you pedalling away on the infernal machine in OT, the fretsaw thing. What are you making? A jigsaw?

Philip Apparently they send them to a Children's Home when they're finished. God help the poor little buggers who get mine.

Tony It looks like hard work.

Philip Can't keep it up for long, not yet. Have to stop and rest.

Tony Yes, I could hear Hitler ranting at you. (*In an accent*) "Philip, why have you stopped? Do you want to be taken out and shot?"

Philip Does Kathy do OT? I haven't seen her there.

Tony She's in the Light Workshop. Playing games like Scrabble, drawing, setting type ... besides her speech, the fine movements of her right hand are affected. Things to make her use it, I suppose. What we've come to. Grown men and women, playing games, making jigsaws, and rocking horses.

Philip What brought you here, Tony? What was it? An accident?

Tony No. I'd been a bit off colour. Flu probably, didn't bother to call the doctor. Anyway, woke up in the night with stomach ache. Stumbled along to the bathroom, half asleep. Sat on the throne. When I went to stand up, the legs gave way, fell on the floor, couldn't get up again. There was me, lying there, yelling for my wife, helpless as a baby. Very embarrassing.

Philip I know the feeling. Soon after I was taken to hospital, I became paraplegic. Somehow I fell out of bed. Same thing, calling for help, and thinking no one would ever hear me. Anyway sorry ...

Tony My wife finally woke up, and came running in. Thank God I hadn't locked the door, or I'd be there yet. Panic. Doctor. Ambulance. Hospital. Finally turned out to be transverse myelitis.

Philip Don't know that one.

Tony No one knows the cause, but it seems to arise from a viral infection. A transverse section of the spinal cord dies, and usually results in paraplegia. They can't predict the degree of recovery, no one can tell how much of the spinal cord has died, but they claim it's never one hundred per cent. Well. I'm going to prove the gloomy bastards wrong. Back on the road, fighting fit, and up theirs, that's me.

Philip What do you sell?

Tony Electrical goods, work for a firm of wholesalers. It's a cut throat business, but I enjoy it. They're keeping it open for me and so they should. I'm bloody good.

Philip Meantime, they're paying you, I suppose.

Tony Yes, but only the basic salary, and the bills don't stop pouring in. My wife's found a job, but she can only work part time, our little girl's just a toddler. It helps, but if I don't get back into harness soon . . . we've got a hell of a big mortgage.

Philip At least, you've got something coming in. Nothing for me except state sickness benefit.

Tony I thought everybody got sick pay these days.

Philip I'm freelance. Self-employed. So far, I've got by because there was some money owing to me. Once that's gone, it's sell the flat time, if I can't get back to work.

Tony How come you can walk if you were paraplegic?

Philip The operation I had restored movement.

Tony I wish there was an operation for mine.

Philip Like you, they were cagey about the degree of recovery. There's been some nerve damage.

Tony Someone said nerves regenerate at the rate of one millimetre a day. I reckon if mine was about there . . . (*He puts a hand to his lower back to where he imagines the approximate level was*) . . . it ought to be getting down to my legs pretty soon.

Philip Who told you that? A millimetre a day?

Tony A fellow in the ward. Why?

Philip Nothing.

Tony Come on. You've heard different. What?

Philip It probably varies . . .

Tony (*insistent*) Never mind the soft soap. Who did you talk to?

Philip The consultant.

Tony Well? And?

Philip He said a centimetre a month would be a lot. Even if they did regenerate.

Tony takes in the required new measurements

Tony Well, OK, it'll be about three times as long. (*Mentally calculating*) You've just wrecked my schedule.

Philip I could have got it wrong . . . anyway, you can get an orange disc for your car, park anywhere, manage that way for a while.

Tony Oh, yes, terrific! Sod that. Back on my own two feet, once the old nerves connect up, you'll see. Well, I'm off. Five minutes, and you can have the wash-basin. (*He wheels himself towards the door. He murmurs as he goes*) One centimetre a month, let's see . . .

Kathy comes in

Tony passes her

Good night, Kathy.

Kathy Good night.

Tony goes

Kathy is looking round

Philip Lost something?

Kathy No. I . . . (*She crosses to the chair on which she was sitting, picks up her cassette recorder and book, moves to Philip, shows him recorder*) This.

Philip Feel like having a try at it?

Kathy No.

Philip Keep me company then.

Kathy Yes . . . all right. (*She sits at the table*)

Philip Nice flowers.

Kathy Yes.

Philip Your room must look like a florist's shop.

Kathy I threw them away.

Philip Why?

Kathy I always do.

Philip I thought . . . well, you gave the impression, that you and he . . .

Kathy I know.

Philip What's changed?

Kathy Us. Both.

Philip I'm sorry it's . . . there's no reason why you should tell me.

Kathy I have. I wanted to. You talk to me. You have been . . . kind.

Philip (*a smile*) I'm not sure I'm a very kind person. It's selfish, really. I like your company.

Kathy The others, I . . . pretend. It's easier . . . not to explain.

Philip He must still care about you.

Kathy In a way. A different way.

Philip How?

A look from Kathy

How different?

Kathy He was driving . . . he wasn't hurt . . . he says often, it is not his fault . . . I tell him it doesn't matter, whose fault . . . to him, though, I think it does . . . but he cannot . . . look at it . . . (*Shaking her head*) . . . something else.

Philip Face it. Accept it.

Kathy He tries to be nice . . . and that hurts . . . the way he tries to be nice . . .

Philip Are you sure that's not just inside your own head?

Kathy I am still a woman. When a man does not want me . . . as a woman . . . I know. He sends flowers . . . he writes nice letters . . . he is sorry for me . . . I don't want . . . (*She gropes for the word*)

Philip Pity? I understand that all right.

Kathy We were together for two years . . . but since this . . . it is over.

Philip I'm sorry. I wish there was something I could do.

Kathy You listen. You hear what I try to say . . . even when I can't say it. You treat me as I am . . . in here . . . not stupid.

Philip I know you're not stupid.

Kathy Now, I have said it . . . about him . . . (*A smile*) But I am not crying.

Philip I know what it's like, when something's broken up. Keeping it to yourself, not wanting to admit it. But I'm not sure I could have gone through all that in this place.

Kathy Sometimes, I have thought . . . it would be nice . . . to be dead.

Philip (*trying to jolly her out of it*) Come on, you don't mean that. I wouldn't like it for a start. I'd have no one to talk to.

Kathy begins to laugh

Kathy (*still laughing*) No one to talk to . . .

Philip Kathy, don't, please. Stop it. (*Loudly*) I'm sorry. (*He levers himself to his feet*)

But Kathy cannot stop laughing, although it is unnatural, and in fact she is deeply distressed

Kathy (*laughing*) You are sorry. He is sorry. You think I want that? Keep it. Talk to someone else. Go away.

Philip Kathy, please. I didn't mean to upset you . . .

Kathy (*overlapping*) Go away! Go away! Go away! Go away!

Philip decides that this is beyond him, and limps away in search of help as quickly as possible (not very quickly)

Kathy continues to laugh, although in spasms as she becomes breathless

We hear Philip's voice receding, as he speaks, off

Philip (*off*) Colin. Colin. Have you seen Mary anywhere? Mary the nurse. Well, where is she, do you know?

Kathy's laughter dies away, leaving her unutterably sad

Automaton-like, she picks up the poetry book, opens it, moves forward, faces the audience, as if she were a little girl on the school hall stage

Kathy (*reading from the book*) To the Virgins, to Make Much of Time. By Robert Herrick.

(*She reads the above as if to herself. Then she lowers the book, crosses her hands in front of her, and recites the poem. She achieves it. But it is an achievement, painful, almost heartbreaking to watch*)

(*Reciting*)

Gather ye Rose-buds while ye may,
Old Time is still a flying:
And this same flower that smiles today,
Tomorrow will be dying.

The glorious Lamp of Heaven, the Sun,
The higher he's a getting;
The sooner will his Race be run,
And nearer he's to Setting.

That Age is best, which is the first,
When Youth and Blood are warmer;
But being spent, the worse, and worst
Times still succeed the former.

Then be not coy, but use your time;
And while ye may, go marry:
For having lost but once your prime,
You may for ever tarry.

CURTAIN

PROLOGUE TO SCENE 1, ACT II

Dialogue from loudspeakers

Nurse Hullo, Len. You're back early.

Len Yes, well, my son reckons what with the kids' bedtime and everything, it's best if he brings me back in time for tea. That way, there's no rush.

Nurse Are you all right, Len?

Len As right as I am after any weekend.

Nurse Didn't it go well?

Len Not especially. And to cap it all . . . I'll tell you Mary, after my Sunday lunch, I sit with those kids watching the telly, waiting for my son to say, "Ready, Dad?", and I want to cry—knowing I've got to come back to this place.

Nurse (*after slight pause*) You know about your appointments tomorrow?

Len Yes.

Nurse We do understand, Len.

Len I wish I did. I wish I knew what it was all about.

ACT II

Room Six. 7.30 a.m. Monday. Week 5

Tony, Douglas, Len and Philip are in bed and asleep. A varied selection of heavy breathing, whistles, and snores. Tony and Douglas have bed cradles over their legs. Douglas's left arm rests on a pillow. Len has a night urine bag hung on the bed frame

This overture continues in the darkened room for a while, and then the Nurse opens the door and switches the light on

Nurse 'Morning, everybody. Good morning. Time to wake up unless you gentlement have decided to miss breakfast.

The four men come round slowly, four drowsy automata. The Nurse is carrying the gear for a urine sample, sealed to keep it sterile. She places it on Len's bedside locker

Tony I'll have mine in bed.
Nurse You'll be lucky. (*She glances at the half full urine bottle on the locker beside Tony's bed*)

Philip What's the time?
Tony Oh, Christ ... (*More awake now, he has felt his sheets with one hand. He indicates the urine bottle*) Sorry, Mary. Spilt some. Must have been half asleep.
Nurse We'll change the sheets. Not to worry.

Douglas sits up too. He gropes for his ortholon splint, which is on his locker to the left-hand side of his bed. Right-handed, he slips it on his left leg, and secures it, after putting on his socks. This done, he sits on the edge of this bed, takes off his pyjama trousers, pulls on his trousers, puts his shoes on, all right-handed, of course

Meanwhile—

Nurse Len. Are you awake? (*She moves to Len's bed*) Len. Wake up.
Len Mm.

The Nurse exits

Philip God, it's half past seven.
Douglas What?

Philip puts slippers on, gets hold of his two sticks, reaches for his dressing gown, slips it on, and leaves the room, heading for the bathroom

Tony (*about Philip's uneven progress—the line sung to a familiar tune*) Skip to the loo, my darling.

The Nurse enters

During her absence the four men have more or less come awake, stretching and making early morning noises, including "good mornings" etc

Nurse (*to Len*) Urine sample this morning.
Len Yes, OK.
Nurse And it's enema day.
Len Let me have another go with the suppositories, Mary. Come on. Perhaps it'll be all right this time. I don't like enemas.
Nurse There are lots of things we all don't like.
Len (*a grumble into thin air*) It's all right for you.

Douglas, when he has his trousers and vest on, makes his way out to the bathroom

The Nurse returns to Tony

Nurse No sign of sores?
Tony Don't think so.

The Nurse quickly checks his legs for herself

Philip comes back in, gets an electric razor from his locker

Nurse Let's make sure. No. Seems fine.
Tony (*grumpy still about wet sheets*) Oh, good. Made my day.

Philip heads for the wash-basin, the strings of his wash bag between his teeth

Helped by the Nurse, Tony, having already put his track suit top on, puts the trousers on

While this is going on—

I've got a bloody physio session this morning, teaching me to bloody stand. Big deal.

Len straps his day bag just above his left knee, disconnects his catheter from the night bag, connects it to his day bag, ties pyjamas again, crosses to the wash-basin, splashes his face with water perfunctorily, just beating Philip to the wash-basin

Tony Foiled again, Phil.
Nurse You have to be able to stand before you can take a few steps.
Tony When's that going to be?
Nurse When you're ready. Just remember, ten steps makes all the difference.
Tony The difference to what?
Nurse Everything. (*Putting Tony's socks on—*) Ten steps means you can

walk into a friend's flat, into a restaurant. You're not completely confined to your wheelchair.

Douglas comes back, picks up his towel and electric razor, eyes Len and Philip impatiently

Tony Jesus, what a load of crap.
Nurse Thanks very much.
Douglas (*to Len and Philip*) Come on. We haven't got all day.
Tony Ten steps is no use to me. Stuff your ten steps. Hobble through a door, and that's an achievement because I'm not "completely" confined to a wheelchair? Sod that. Not completely, not partly, just hand it back for some other poor bugger, that's me.
Nurse Please yourself. We're short handed this morning, and I've other patients to see to.

The Nurse hurries out, taking Tony's urine bottle

Tony (*calling after her*) So that's why we were late being called is it? (*To himself*) Short handed. Some Florence Nightingale woke up with a hangover and decided to stay in bed.

Tony uses a transfer board to slide sideways into his wheelchair. (One arm of the wheelchair drops down to allow him to do this.) Once in his wheelchair, Tony puts on his gym shoes

Meanwhile, Len has finished. He returns to his bedside locker, picks up the urine sample tray, and goes out with it

Douglas (*as Len moves away*) About time too.

But before Douglas can get to the wash-basin, Philip shuffles sideways to the wash-basin, where he starts to shave

Philip, I like to wash *before* I shave.
Philip You'll have to wait then, won't you, Douglas.
Douglas Oh, really, it's just not good enough. Calling us late ... I detest hurrying in the morning. You don't get a decent shave if you haven't washed first.
Tony Oh, stop moaning.
Douglas Well, it's ridiculous.
Tony Moan, moan, moan.

The Nurse hurries in, carrying two suppositories

Nurse Len's suppositories. (*She places them on Len's bedside locker*) Tell him will you?

The Nurse hurries out again

Tony Yes, ma'am. Whatever you say, ma'am.
Douglas One wash-basin for the four of us ... utterly absurd ...

Tony flicks his towel over his shoulder, picks up his electric razor, wheels himself towards the wash-basin

Tony Right. The important one's ready. Who's going to give way.
Douglas Wait your turn.
Philip Shan't be long.

Tony parks his wheelchair, and waits

Tony Wonder if the papers have arrived yet. First one to finish, get a *Telegraph* for me, OK?

Len comes in

Len, your exploding capsules, over there.
Len Oh, right. She let me have them then, did she? (*He moves to his locker, picks up the two suppositories. Dubiously—*) May as well get it over with, I suppose. Wish me luck (*He moves to go*)
Tony Hey, Len.

Len pauses, looks at him enquiringly

Tony I reckon for all the good those things do, you might as well stuff them up your arse.

Len gives a weak grin and goes

Philip finishes, collects his things, gets hold of his sticks, and then finds that he cannot get past Tony's wheelchair

Philip Tony, back up. I can't pole vault over you.
Tony Why not? You're the fittest man here.
Philip Come on, bugger off!

Tony spins his wheelchair backwards. Philip gets his razor cord tangled in his sticks, tries to shake it free

Tony (*about Philip's antics*) Bloody action man.

As Tony is about to move to the vacant space in front of the wash-basin, Douglas finishes shaving, and moves sideways. Tony makes "revving up" noises

Douglas Oh, go away.
Tony Come on, old son, unless you want to get run over.

Tony gets past, plugs in his electric razor, and starts to shave

Douglas runs the tap, splashes his face vigorously with his right hand, and then under his armpits

Hey, careful. I'll wash myself, thank you.
Douglas You try it with one hand some time.
Tony Oh, poor fellow. You try it from a wheelchair, mate.
Douglas Rush, rush, rush . . . I loathe communal living . . . it's so uncivilised . . . and why? . . . Music and Movement doesn't start until twenty to ten . . . there's nothing to do after breakfast except hang about, anyway . . .
Tony What a happy little soul you are, Douglas. You're supposed to return

from weekend parole cheered and refreshed for the fray. Your better half give you a bad time, did she?

Douglas It was extremely pleasant, thank you. (*He starts to clean his teeth*) That's what got to me ... the contrast ...

Tony switches off his electric razor

Tony Why don't you clean your teeth after breakfast? What's the point in doing it now, except to get on my nerves?

Douglas I like to clean them before ... and after ... breakfast.

Tony Well, get a move on, or all the "Torygraphs" 'll be gone.

Douglas rinses his mouth, moves away, puts on a short-sleeved shirt, right-handed

Hooray.

Tony manoeuvres his wheelchair sideways to the wash-basin, starts to wash

Douglas I keep reminding them about my *Financial Times*. I suppose they'll have forgotten again.

Tony Well, get up there and find out.

Douglas Is yours *The Times*, Philip?

Philip The *Guardian*.

Douglas Really?

Tony He's a closet, radical trendy. Didn't you know?

Douglas Frightful rag. Can't stand all those opinionated people. (*He is squinting into the mirror, brushing his hair*)

Tony Look, voice of sweet reason, what's the point of poncing yourself up? No one's going to fancy you. I get withdrawal symptoms if I don't have my "Torygraph" in time for breakfast.

Douglas moves to the door

And get Len the *Sun*. Then I can look at page three.

Douglas goes

Tony Not that I need anything to turn me on. Something to turn me off might be more to the point. (*Drying his face*) Page three, forget it. You should see my wife in a bikini.

Philip I can imagine.

Tony You've never met her.

Philip I was waiting for my cab when she picked you up on Friday. She's lovely.

Tony Yes, she keeps me on the straight and narrow. Well, all that behind your own front door, why wander?

Len comes in

What? Success already?

Len Haven't tried yet. Thought I'd wait for a while.

Tony Give 'em time to ferment, that's the spirit. Still, I don't think I wish to be in the vicinity when the ooh—aah—ugh takes place.

Tony throws his towel across the room on to his bed, and wheels himself out

Len starts to remove his pyjamas and dress himself. He sits on his bed with his back to the audience when he is changing his trousers—though it might be effective if we could glimpse the urine bag, without seeing the catheter

Len I shall be glad when today's over.

Philip Perhaps it'll be all right this time.

Len What? Oh. I don't mean my bowels. No. Seeing people. The psychiatrist, the social worker ...

Philip What about?

Len Try and sort things out over the weekend, that was the idea. I suppose I did, in a way. Went to see the friend I told you about.

Philip The lady you're going to marry.

Len Was. She's still willing. I'm not.

Philip I thought you were fond of her.

Len It wouldn't do. Not now.

Philip If she's agreeable, why not?

Len Come on, Phil. I've got a permanent catheter ... once a month, they change it for me. Every day, I have to clean it, or I'm liable to get infected. You've seen the carry on I have to go through. (*Pointing*) The bloody bag hanging on the bed at night.

Philip Aren't they considering some sort of operation for you?

Len Not for a year or so.

Philip Well, a year's not so long. You might feel differently then.

Len It wouldn't make any difference Phil, what they do, they resect the muscle at the neck of the bladder, nip a bit out, so the bladder drains freely. I'll still have to wear an appliance, one of those condom things.

Philip Then what's the point of the operation?

Len They reckon you're less liable to infection with an external appliance. I'll still be left with all my tubes and drainage bags. I couldn't inflict all that on someone else.

Philip Have you explained all this to your friend?

Len God, no.

Philip Why don't you? You say she's a nice woman ...

Len She is, but ...

Philip Let her decide. It might not make any difference.

Len It makes a difference to me. I disgust myself. I couldn't share a home with someone, doing all the things I have to do day after day. I couldn't. No.

Philip You might consider trying to get some help ...

Len Who from? Who's going to get everything working again? No one. There's nothing anyone can do.

Philip Talk to the psychiatrist about it. That's what he's there for.

Len He can't change how I feel. Anyway, that's only the half of it. I was hoping my old firm could find some sort of job for me, but they can't and I've sod all put by.

Philip What about compensation?

Len It was my own fault, no one else's. Climbing down from my crane, thinking about something else, slipped, and fell on my back across some baulks of timber. God knows what I shall do with myself. Sit in my flat and look out of the window, I suppose, and there's bugger all to see except the thin air between me and the next tower block.

Philip You could go and live with your son.

Len It's not practical. We went into that. (*Loyally*) See what with the kids growing up, they're going to need the spare room soon, so . . . they're only too glad to have me any time, but as for living there . . . anyway, it's not as though I haven't got a place of my own to go back to. If only I hadn't slipped that day.

Philip Yes, "if only". We all think that, I expect. If only it hadn't happened. If only it hadn't been me.

Len (*a sudden grin*) I hope you had a better weekend than I did. What did you do?

Philip Not much. It was nice to have a couple of days in my own flat again. Phoned a couple of friends, but they were tied up. Walked as much as I could.

Len How far did you manage?

Philip Queensway and back. I live about a quarter of a mile away.

Len Half a mile all told. That's pretty good.

Philip (*a wry smile*) By present standards, yes. You know what Queensway's like, crowded, everyone hurrying along, dashing across the road, running for buses. And there was me on my two sticks, and my big problem was how to get myself those few inches up and down, on and off the pavement. And I thought, it's another world.

Len All the things that bother us, and they don't give it a thought, yes. Not so long ago, if I saw a bloke in a wheelchair, like Tony, I thought, "That's the way he is. Poor sod. Glad it's not me." Never crossed my mind how he might feel about it. (*He looks thoughtful*) Something could be happening. Excuse me. (*He heads for the door*)

Philip You'll be late for breakfast.

Len Let's hope I ain't late for anything else.

Len goes

Philip, who has paused in his dressing while talking to Len, puts his plimsolls on or whatever. (He wears a tracksuit)

The Nurse hurries in, carrying clean sheets, and begins to strip Tony's bed

Philip Len's left his sample.

Nurse (*busy*) Right.

Philip What's going to happen to him, Mary? A job for instance, isn't there some official, the Disabled something.

Nurse The Disabled Resettlement Officer.

Philip Len's pretty active compared with most.

Nurse Only a few years ago, the D.R.O. could find a job for anyone who wanted to work. Not any more. Not these days.

Philip What about retraining?

Nurse Len's too old to be considered for that.

Philip Too old? He can't be more than fifty three, fifty four.
Nurse The retiring age could be reduced in the next ten years or so. Retraining for people of Len's age isn't regarded as cost effective. Too little of their working lives left at the end of it.
Philip It's crazy! Len wants to work.
Nurse Well, I doubt if he ever will again.

The Nurse bundles up the soiled sheets and leaves the clean sheets on the end of the bed, which will be made up later

Nurse Len's a widower. If he had a good family environment to go back to, that'd be the best thing. But while I expect his son's quite fond of his father, he doesn't want Dad living with him. So Len will receive community care for the rest of his life. The village, which looks after its own, that's the analogy.
Philip I doubt if his tower block much resembles a village.
Nurse He'll see the social worker, the health visitor, the chiropodist. He'll receive Meals on Wheels. He'll have access to Community Centres, and Day Centres for the Disabled where he can play draughts and dominoes, and vegetate out of sight. (*She moves to Len's bedside locker and picks up his urine sample*)
Philip That makes this place seem a waste of time.
Nurse We do good work here. Some, a good many, improve a lot, and can still fulfil themselves afterwards. That's worthwhile. Len happens to be one of the unlucky ones.
Philip That's not bad luck. It's bloody wrong.

Len walks in

Len No luck. False alarm. (*About the urine sample in the Nurse's hand*) Oh, you've got it.
Nurse They'll be serving breakfast.

The Nurse goes

Len and Philip move towards the door

Kathy, passing, pauses

Len Morning, Kathy.
Kathy Good morning.

Len moves on and out of sight

Kathy lingers, looking at Philip

Nice weekend?
Philip (*offhand*) Fine.
Kathy Philip, I came to ... (*She breaks off*)
Philip Yes? What?

Kathy consults a slip of paper on which she has written down the important word

Kathy To apologize.

It is a peace offering Philip is only too glad to accept

Philip Oh, Kathy, you don't have to. I understand. How was your weekend?
Kathy All right. Except ...
Philip Except what?
Kathy No one to talk to.
Philip Me too. Well ... breakfast?
Kathy Yes.
Philip Right. Let's go.

The Lights fade to Black-out

PROLOGUE TO SCENE 2

Dialogue from loudspeakers

Philip What about it, Len? Are you on?
Len Too right, mate.
Tony That's three. You Kathy?
Kathy Yes, please.
Philip I've already asked her.
Tony Provided there's no ABC. Scintillating conversation instead OK?
Kathy (*amused*) Yes ... scin ... conversation ... what you said.
Tony Try sparkling.
Kathy Sparkling ... I can say that ...
Philip Douglas?
Tony Douglas never sparkles. He could send for his Mercedes though. Doug?
Douglas I'd rather not. I always speak to my wife.
Tony Stand her up for once. Make her wonder.
Douglas No, thanks.
Tony All right, be a miserable old sod. Who's going to phone?
Philip I will.
Tony Right, well do it now. Let's get going.

SCENE 2

The Patients' Lounge. 9.30 p.m. Thursday. Week 6

Douglas is sitting, reading the Financial Times. *He has it nicely folded for this one-handed operation*

The Nurse is tidying chairs

From the corridor is heard the bang of a door and general laughter. Douglas looks at the door. The approaching quartet (off) are Philip, Kathy, Len and Tony

The Nurse goes to investigate

Nurse (*as she goes out of sight*) Someone's had a good time.
Tony (*off*) Give us a kiss, darling.
Len (*off*) Throw a bucket of cold water over him, Mary.

Which seems madly funny to those in the corridor, if not to Douglas

Tony (*off*) Oh, you should have been with us, Mary.
Nurse (*off*) I think I'm glad I wasn't . . . (*Receding*) Don't forget to collect
your drugs.
Tony (*off*) What? The night is young.

Tony wheels himself through the door

(*Singing*) And if you want to go dancing, dear . . .

Kathy, Philip and Len come in as well

*They are all in light hearted good spirits, partly due to an unaccustomed, if
modest, alcohol intake, mostly because of a "normal" evening out. Wearing
beautific smiles, they look at Douglas*

Douglas stares back at them bootfaced

Why, if it isn't Douglas.

Mirth begins to simmer in all of them

Fancy seeing you here.

Little bubbles of suppressed laughter

Douglas gazes at them unmoved and motionless

How's the stockmarket, sir? (*Beginning to laugh out loud*) Been worrying
me all evening how my shares are doing.

*All are laughing out loud now, except Douglas who continues to gaze at them
without moving*

Philip Tony.
Tony What?
Philip (*about Douglas*) He's not moving.
Tony Gad. Kathy, fetch a doctor, if you can find one anywhere in this
establishment.

Tony wheels himself close to Douglas

Cancel that. Call the undertaker. Fellow's passed away where he sat. Poor
old Doug.
Philip He wasn't so bad.
Kathy I liked him.
Tony I thought he was a shocker.
Len Mustn't speak ill of the dead.
Tony Why not? Always cleaning his teeth . . . getting in the way . . .
Kathy He had a kind face, though.

Tony What? The master of men? Look at him. "Ruthless shit" written all over him.

Philip The granite jaw ...

Tony Ice cold eyes ...

Len Ruddy complexion ...

Tony He was a secret drinker, you know.

Philip No, I think someone's embalmed him already.

Tony Oh, I'm going to wet myself in a minute.

Douglas Well, I gather you enjoyed yourselves.

Tony My God, the resurrection. It's a miracle. Do I hear angel voices?

Len That's the telly.

Which sets them off again, briefly after which they wear the satisfied smiles of those who have made a notable expedition and survived. Like all such explorers, they want to recount their experiences

Philip, Kathy and Len make their way to chairs and sit down

Douglas Where did you go?

Tony Well, we asked the cab driver ...

Philip A pub with no steps ...

Len And a loo off the bar ...

Tony He suggested ... where was it?

Kathy *The Green Man.*

Len Nice place, panelled bar, good drop of lager ... po-faced landlord though ...

Philip When we arrive, me on sticks ...

Tony Me in my wheelchair, Kathy speechless ...

Kathy I was not.

Tony All right, dopey.

Philip He looked at us as though we were being carted off in the plain van to the funny farm.

Tony With Len in charge.

Douglas I'm not surprised if you behaved like this.

Tony We were models of decorum, sir.

More laughter

(*Remembering something*) Here, I must tell you. The time came for me to go to the loo. Well, I got in there all right, but my wheelchair wouldn't fit into the W.C. So I looked at the urinal ... (*He mimes the actions of grasping the urinal for support and standing up*) ... got as close as I could, and stood up. (*He begins to laugh*) And then I thought, "What do I do now?" I'm stuck there. Stranded. Because I need to get my flies undone, and there's no way without a third hand, and I haven't got a third hand. Finally I got it worked out. (*Craning his neck forward, birdlike*) I leaned my head against the wall, and managed to snatch my zip down. But when I'd finished I couldn't pull it up again ...

Philip I came in at that point. I thought he'd been a long time ...

Tony I wanted him to send for Kathy, and let her do it, but he wouldn't.

Kathy You'd be lucky!
Tony Oh, it was a good evening. It really was.

Kathy tries to stifle a giggle

Don't. Not again. I shall have an accident.

Which makes Kathy worse

When it was Kathy's turn, Len had been acting as waiter, but she wanted to go and get the drinks herself. We were all having something different, so she memorized it, went across to the bar, muttering under her breath ... a pint of lager, a whisky and water ...
Philip She'd have got it right, if it hadn't been for you.
Tony I shouted out, told her I'd changed my mind, and wanted a Campari soda instead. She forgot the lot, just stood there, with her mouth open like a goldfish, and the barman thinking, "God, we've got a right one here ..."

Kathy, although laughing in sympathy, is shaking her head

Kathy No, not then. Later.
Tony When?
Kathy When the man came to collect the glasses ...
Tony Oh, yes, the po-faced landlord. I asked him if he'd heard the one about the blind man who walked into Woolworths swinging his guide dog around his head, and the manager said "Can I help you, sir?" And the blind man said "No thanks. Just having a look round."

Douglas stares at him, bootfaced

And the po-faced landlord stared at me like a decayed cod. Just like you. Good job wet blanket here turned us down. He'd have killed the evening stone dead.

Len has been patting his bag anxiously, and now stands up

Len Here we go again. Excuse me.
Tony Downing pints of lager all night, what do you expect?
Len (*as he goes*) I like lager. It reaches the parts other beers cannot reach.

Len goes

Tony Here's one more up your street, Doug. "Do you talk to your wife when you're making love?" "Only if there's a telephone handy."

Douglas lifts his left arm into position and stands up

Time to clean your teeth is it? Off you go, then.
Douglas I have to phone my wife. The number was engaged earlier.
Tony Perhaps she takes the phone off the hook when she's ... taking the dog for a walk. Taking the dog for a walk, Doug.

Unexpectedly, Douglas smiles

Douglas Yes.

Douglas makes his way out

(*On the move—chuckling*) Taking the dog for a walk. That's very good.

Douglas goes

Tony He's bloody potty. What did he think I meant? The mind boggles. (*He sighs comfortably, looks at his watch*) Well perhaps I'll go and bag the wash-basin. It made a change, didn't it.
Kathy I enjoyed it.
Tony Hang on, Kathy, I'll have a Campari soda instead.

Kathy is able to laugh at herself now, and does so

(*Grinning*) See you then. I'm being tactful, you realize that.

Tony wheels himself towards the door

(*As he moves away*) Don't do anything I wouldn't do, you two, and by Heaven that leaves the field wide open. (*Singing*) "I'm in the mood for dancing . . ." (*He bumps into wall*) Whoops . . .

Tony goes

Philip and Kathy look at each other comfortably. Philip stifles a yawn

Kathy Tired?
Philip M'm. A little. They've put me on something different in OT. The treadle. (*He moves his hands up and down indicating the movement of his feet on the treadle*) It's a killer. Still, another weekend soon. Two days off.
Kathy What . . . do you do? See friends?
Philip One or two. I haven't as many as I once thought.
Kathy Why not?
Philip I was like most people, I suppose. The wonders of modern medicine . . . a sort of received myth that if you become ill, there's a drug to cure it, or an operation, and after that, you're fully restored. Hey presto, good as new.
Kathy Yes, I know that . . . belief . . . but you were saying . . . about friends.
Philip When I was rushed into hospital, the get well cards arrived in shoals. All those people who cared. Visitors too, one after another. I came round after the operation, and I thought "Right, that's over. When do I get out?" Another myth. For days I was too weak to move. Nurses used to turn me over every two hours, to prevent bed sores. Weeks later, I was still in hospital and the visitors had dwindled to about four or five. The rest, I suppose they thought, "He's had his operation, he must be cured. Done my bit. That's that."
Kathy Four or five . . . real friends . . . is good.
Philip Yes, reality dawns all round. Still it gave me time to think about my mistakes. Things that have gone wrong.
Kathy Things wrong . . . in your own life?
Philip My marriage went sour when maybe it needn't have done. I'm a working animal, my work came first. I think she felt shut out.
Kathy She must have known . . . the man you were . . .

Philip I'm not saying it was all me. I just feel I might have been more considerate, understanding, whatever.

Kathy I'm sure . . . there were women . . . after that.

Philip One or two. No one close though, nothing like that.

Kathy I think perhaps . . . it was you . . . made sure . . . it was never close.

Philip We've got off the track again.

Kathy It's good . . . talking to someone . . . properly . . .

Philip At first, editors rang up, there was this feature, that assignment. Hurry up and get better. I was needed. Well, I'm still out of action, and other people have taken over those assignments. The world hasn't come to a stop after all, just because I'm not available. (*A smile at Kathy*) Not much of a discovery. We've all experienced that blinding revelation.

Kathy Yes . . . someone else is teaching . . . my class . . . and I think . . . but it is my class . . . (*Pause*) . . . the . . . thing you had . . .

Philip Tumour.

Kathy Was it sudden?

Philip I'd had a lot of back pain. I thought it was an old slipped disc playing up. Took pain killers and kept going. I did have a check up, but nothing showed up. It really hit me when I was in Cairo. Quite indescribable pain, had to be helped on to the plane. When I got back, I saw a neuro-surgeon. He did a myelogram. There was a very faint shadow, which he thought was a tumour on the spinal chord. He was right.

Kathy Suppose the . . . tumour . . . had been . . . discovered earlier, would you have been so . . . affected?

Philip Half the world gets back pain, the symptoms weren't typical, medicine isn't the exact science we like to believe. For instance, the nice-looking woman in a wheelchair, Wendy, all there, but nearly helpless. You know why? Migraine.

Kathy What?

Philip Bad migraine. They couldn't find the cause, and finally decided to try some new test which involved a general anaesthetic. When she came round, she was like she is now. Quadraplegic.

Kathy That is . . . awful . . .

Philip No one's fault, she's been told, but very occasionally something goes wrong. She must just accept it. Wendy says she's damned if she's going to accept it. "You and your bloody test put me in this wheelchair," she tells them, "and now you can bloody well get me out of it." They tell her to be reasonable and face the facts.

Kathy Reasonable!

Philip That woman's courage . . . I don't know if it's crazy, or useless, but I admire her.

Kathy Will you hear me say the alphabet again?

Philip Now?

Kathy Like her . . . I don't feel . . . reasonable.

Philip All right.

Kathy It will be right . . . I can . . . feel it . . . I need to be . . . able . . . once . . . just once . . . and after that . . .

Philip I know.

Kathy Don't help me.

Philip gives Kathy an encouraging smile

OK.

A few moments, while Kathy psyches herself up for the big moment. Then she begins, steadily

A ... B ... C ... D ... E ... F ... G ... H ... I ... J ... K ... (*Pause*) ... J ... K ... L ... M ... N ... (*Longer pause*) ... O ... O ... P ... Q ... R ... S (*Long pause*) ... T ... U ... (*Long pause*) ... R ... S ... T ... U ... (*Pause*) ... V ... U ... V ... V ...

This time, the pause drags on. Kathy's face shows her inner frustration

... U ... V ... V ...

Kathy stops again, confronting defeat. Suddenly she hammers the table fiercely

Fuck! Fuck! Fuck!

Kathy stares at Philip, her face rigid with frustration. Philip's lips twitch in a smile

Philip You said that last bit beautifully.

Slowly, Kathy too begins to smile. Her amusement grows, but it is natural amusement. She reaches out and takes Philip's hand gratefully

The Lights fade to Black-out

PROLOGUE TO SCENE 3

Dialogue from loudspeakers

The Dining Room. Breakfast

Tony Morning, Kathy.
Kathy Good morning.
Tony Room for a little one beside you?
Kathy Yes.
Tony Pass the old bran what's-it, will you? Ta. How was your weekend?
Kathy Not good.
Tony Mine had its ups and downs too. More down than up.
Kathy Sorry?
Tony Doesn't matter. Private joke. Is there any more milk?
Kathy Here.
Tony Thanks. You looked dead chirpy when you set off on Friday.
Kathy I know but ... that changed ...
Tony Hey, you're not going to cry on me, are you?
Kathy No ... that is past ... I think ...

Tony That's good. Here, see if you can crack nine down for me. I can't get the damn thing.

SCENE 3

Speech Therapy. 2.15 p.m. Monday. Week 7

Kathy and the Speech Therapist

Kathy has to think during these exercises—she is deliberately being made to work hard

Speech Therapist Zero.
Kathy Nothing.
Speech Therapist Fair.
Kathy Blonde.
Speech Therapist Yes. Another meaning? In dealing with someone.
Kathy Honest.
Speech Therapist Good. Drowsy.
Kathy Sleepy.
Speech Therapist Implore.
Kathy Ask.
Speech Therapist It's stronger than that, isn't it? A synonym. A word which means the same. If you implore someone, you . . . ?
Kathy Beg them.
Speech Therapist Beg, excellent. Right, now we'll do the one where I give you the definition, and you tell me what the word is. Ready?
Kathy Yes.
Speech Therapist   Good fortune, chance.
Kathy Luck.
Speech Therapist Animals with strong incisor and no canine teeth.
Kathy Squirrels.
Speech Therapist Good. Now the generic name. What that group of animals is called. (*Long pause*) Well, that's a difficult one. Never mind . . .
Kathy Rodents.
Speech Therapist Very good. Try another hard one. Extreme scarcity of food in a district.
Kathy Oh . . . I know that . . . I know it . . .
Speech Therapist No hurry.
Kathy People starving . . . oh . . .
Speech Therapist Shall I give you the first letter?
Kathy No . . . it's . . . (*She breaks off, stumped*)
Speech Therapist Let's come back to that one later.
Kathy Famine. That's it. Famine.
Speech Therapist You're doing extremely well, Kathy. You've improved so much.
Kathy Not sufficient . . .

Speech Therapist Well, the degree of recovery acceptable to the patient varies with each individual, but you have made a great deal of progress.

Kathy I wanted to go back to teaching ...

Speech Therapist (*gently*) I did warn you ...

Kathy I know ... I've been told ... I can't. I still can't do ... joined up writing ... and they say ... in class, I couldn't ... manage, well enough.

Speech Therapist Do you think they're wrong to say that?

Kathy Not yet ... perhaps ...

Speech Therapist It's not always possible for patients with your condition to return to their former jobs, especially if the work makes the kind of demands which teaching does. You may have to adjust to that.

Kathy I don't want to adjust. They offered me another job ...

Speech Therapist Doing what?

Kathy As a helper ... in a Play School.

Speech Therapist How does that appeal to you?

Kathy It was a great ... defeat.

Speech Therapist It must have been a disappointment, I know, but at least you'd be working with children.

Kathy As a helper ... not even in charge ... only a helper ...

Speech Therapist Your treatment won't stop when you leave here, Kathy. You'll go on having speech therapy as an out-patient. You might improve enough to take on more responsibility in due course.

Kathy When?

Speech Therapist I don't know. You've made a good recovery so far. You could go on improving, but to what degree and for how long, I can't tell, no one can.

Kathy You think I should take it ... become a helper ...

Speech Therapist That has to be your decision. It's a job. It is with children. It's not what you want most, but it's something.

Kathy's expression is unresponsive

Kathy I did not say ... the wrong word ... to take it would be ... not a disappointment ... it would be ... a defeat.

The Lights fade to Black-out

PROLOGUE TO SCENE 4

Dialogue from loudspeakers

Nurse Ready for your bath, Tony?

Tony (*in bad humour*) No, I'm not. Why are all you nurses obsessed with my private parts?

Nurse In this job, you don't even notice.

Tony That's right, make me feel good, cheer me up.

Nurse Do you need it?

Tony What do you think? I do all the physio, I play bloody silly games in the gym, I get individual treatment, they strap weights on my legs and I try and lift them ... and I still can't take one step, never mind the ten you were on about.

Nurse It takes time, Tony.

Tony Malcolm was discharged last week.

Nurse I know. What about it?

Tony That makes me the oldest inhabitant of this rotten place, that's what.

SCENE 4

Physiotherapy. 3.30 p.m. Tuesday. Week 7

Tony is in his wheelchair, which is close to the wall bars

Douglas is practising walking

Philip is standing, keeping his balance by lightly touching the Physiotherapist's fingertips with his left hand. His weight is on his left leg, and he is tapping a football round himself with his right foot. For him, this is not an easy exercise, and he sways, and "loses" the football once or twice, when the Physiotherapist taps it back to him

Physiotherapist (*during this*) Just a light touch to keep your balance ... don't lean on me, I'm not going to support you ... that's better ...

Philip (*losing football*) Sorry ...

Physiotherapist (*tapping it back to him with one foot*) Here you are ... try and control it ...

Tony Oh, highly fancy footwork. Another Kevin Keegan in the making, there.

The Physiotherapist appears to have eyes in the back of her head, and berates Douglas while continuing her gyrations

Physiotherapist Douglas, you're not concentrating. I'm not going to let you walk like that, and you needn't think I am.

Douglas What's wrong?

Physiotherapist You know perfectly well what's wrong. How many times have I told you to take more weight on that left leg? But no, you'd rather walk any old how, wouldn't you.

Douglas (*stung*) Now look here, young woman.

Tony The worm turns. Rebellion.

Douglas There's nothing I want more than to walk like a human being again.

Physiotherapist Well, why don't you put into practice what I've been telling you during the sessions? You have to do it for yourself. I can't do it for you. Now, come on, again, and *think* about it this time. More weight on that left leg. It'll carry you perfectly well.

Bootfaced, Douglas starts off again. This time, his walking is even, although it is a slow measured pace

That's better. That's much better. You see, you can do it when you put
your mind to it. Well done!

*Douglas, his back to the Physiotherapist, facing the audience, mouths "Well
done" in silent irony*

All right Philip, that wasn't bad at all.
Tony (*a mutter*) Teacher's pet.

*The Physiotherapist takes her hand away from Philip's, picks up the single
walking stick which he is using now, and hands it to him*

Physiotherapist The balance board now.

*Philip walks towards the rectangular balance board, which is beside some wall
bars*

Tony pretends to have a heart attack and die. No one takes any notice

*The Physiotherapist watches Philip walk away. Philip's left leg and hip are
much weaker than his right, and he walks with a pronounced limp*

Philip, turn round and walk back towards me.

Philip complies, under the Physiotherapist's scrutiny

Try not to limp.
Philip Can't help it.

The Physiotherapist backs away so that he can keep coming towards her

Physiotherapist You're coming off the inside of your left foot. Heel, ball of
the foot, follow straight through.

*Philip does his best to comply with the instruction, as he follows the
Physiotherapist*

Tony Walkies.
Philip Sit!!

*The Physiotherapist circles backwards, in a path taking her towards the
balance board*

Physiotherapist (*dubious*) That's a bit better, but not much. Your walking
was better with two sticks.
Philip (*firmly*) I'm not going back to two, Helen, forget it.
Physiotherapist I don't want you to get into bad habits. Douglas, sit on the
stool, please. (*To Philip*) We'd better concentrate on the balance board
more, exercise those muscles which aren't working properly. That's why
your balance is so poor. (*She turns away*)

*Philip hooks his stick on the wall bars, grips them, climbs on to the balance
board, facing the wall bars. The board is placed so that his feet are "across"
the curved section underneath the board. When in position, he gingerly releases
his hold on the wall bars, but his rocking movements are coarse, and he has to
dab at the wall bars now and then to save himself*

Douglas, meanwhile, has sat on a stool, and has already succeeded in straightening the fingers of his left hand, by using his right hand

The Physiotherapist straightens his left arm for him, checks his left hand fingers

Good. Right, off you go.

Douglas begins his "hand above head" exercise

The Physiotherapist wheels the full length mirror and positions it facing Tony

Tony Hooray. A bit of action at last.
Physiotherapist So brace yourself, Tony.

Tony releases the step of his wheelchair, and the Physiotherapist lifts him to his feet, where he stands, supporting himself by holding on to the wall bars

Get your balance, first of all.

Tony does his best

Philip, lurching about like that is doing no good at all. Get your balance and then hold it. (*Watching as Philip attempts to do so*) Hold it ... don't stick your behind out, stand up straight. Start again. Get your balance ... now control the board with your feet, not by wobbling to and fro, that's what exercises those muscles.

Philip manages it for a few seconds, and is then obliged to grab the wall bars for support

Philip Sorry ...
Physiotherapist Try again, and remember what I've told you. When you feel the muscles tiring, turn the board round, and do it the other way.

Philip carries on on his own. At some point, if desired, he steps off the board and steps back on it so that his feet are parallel to the curved section underneath the board, and continues. The second exercise is easier for him, and he is steadier

The Physiotherapist concentrates on Tony

All right, Tony, have you got your balance?
Tony I think so.
Physiotherapist Move your weight from one side to the other ... left ... right ... back again ... a nice, steady movement ...

The Physiotherapist is behind Tony, both facing the mirror. Her arms are underneath his armpits, but not supporting him, and she points at the mirror as she speaks for emphasis

... good ... still now ... hand off the bars ... your hips aren't forward enough ...

All this is an immense strain for Tony, needing all the grim effort and concentration he can muster push your bottom forward ...

Tony Careful, woman. Don't tempt me.

Physiotherapist ... push it forward ... come on ... check yourself in the mirror ... you're not looking in the mirror ... let's have those shoulders back a little further ... more ... that's it ... keep those hips forward ... all right, rest for a minute.

Tony returns his hand to the wall bars, as she releases him. Breathes deeply once or twice

Tony How about letting me try a few steps?

Physiotherapist Until you're able to get the balance right, you're not going to be able to walk.

Tony (*about Philip*) What about Shakin' Stevens there? His balance is terrible, he can walk.

Physiotherapist You know it's not the same, Tony.

Tony (*with quiet despair*) Come on, Helen. Mary gave me that stuff about ten steps makes all the difference. It doesn't, not to me, but if I could do ten, I could do twenty, if I could do twenty, I could do fifty ...

Physiotherapist (*also quietly*) It doesn't necessarily follow. I'm sorry, but it doesn't.

Tony It might. It could do. But even to get to ten, I've got to take one sometime. I've got to make a start.

And Tony tries to take one step. But his effort comprises attempting to "throw" his right hip forward, as it were, the leg does not follow, it crumples under him and he starts to fall

The Physiotherapist, ever alert, is moving even as he tries, and catches him as he falls forward

Oh, Christ ...

Douglas stands up from his stool, alarmed

Douglas Helen ...

Philip Do you need a hand?

Philip, looks round, steps off the balance board

Physiotherapist (*to Douglas and Philip*) It's all right, Tony slipped, that's all. Get on with your exercises. Nothing to worry about.

Douglas and Philip resume

Tony has now got hold of the bars, as the Physiotherapist eases him into a standing position

(*Quietly*) Tony, I'm not going to allow you to try and walk until you can do the balance exercises, so don't you ever do anything silly like that again.

Tony Yes, teacher, three bags full, teacher.

Physiotherapist You'd better sit and get your breath back.

Tony I don't want to sit. I do nothing but bloody sit!!

Physiotherapist Quite sure you're all right?

Tony I'm OK. Let go ...

Physiotherapist (*resuming previous position behind him*) Right ... shoulders back ... hips further forward ... hand off ... steady ... watch those shoulders ... look at yourself in the mirror ... don't let your hips go back ... push your bottom forward ...

The Lights fade to Black-out

PROLOGUE TO SCENE 5

Dialogue from loudspeakers

Nurse Philip, you're seeing Doctor Davidson, nine o'clock Monday morning.

Philip Right.

Nurse After that, Mrs Reed at twelve, and Mr Ward at three.

Philip (*drily*) Busy day. OK.

Nurse Douglas, your appointment with Doctor is at nine fifteen. Len ...

Len Sister's told me mine.

Nurse Right. Has anyone seen Andrew? He's not in his room.

Tony Never mind about Andrew, what about me?

Nurse Just the usual review for you, Tony.

Tony Why is it I always get left out of everything?

SCENE 5

Patients' Lounge. 6.45 p.m. Monday. The last week

Philip and Douglas are sitting together

Douglas I gather the doctor's indulging in some wholesale weeding out.

Philip Yes.

Douglas looks at his left arm, which he still has to move about with his right hand

Douglas It's no better. Useless. An object. Doesn't even seem as if it belongs to me.

Philip I expect they'd say it was no worse.

Douglas I didn't think that was quite the idea. He told me I'll never be able to drive again.

Philip Your walking's improved a lot.

Douglas I walk like an old man. From the chairman down, they'll be giving me sideways looks.

Philip Let them. You can do your job.

Douglas I have perceptual problems as well, due to the loss of the left half of the visual fields. If I'm not careful, I bump into things.

Philip I didn't realize that. You cover it up well.

Douglas Try to. Get confused sometimes, though. And there'll be keen eyes, watching. My company is full of ambitious young men. Young lions. Just waiting. Civilization's version of tooth and claw.

Douglas adjusts his left arm and stands up

Words will bring a man down though. I can hear them now. "Douglas isn't the same man . . . he's not up to it any more . . . he should retire early, take things easy . . . for his own good. . ." That's how it'll be. Put out to grass. All the work, all the effort—all for nothing.

Douglas makes his measured way out, passing Kathy as she comes in and joins Philip

Philip Scrabble tonight?

Kathy If you like.

Philip has the Scrabble set ready on the table

Philip May as well. Good practice.

Philip offers Kathy the bag. She takes her letters and starts to set them up— favouring her left hand

Use your right hand.

Kathy I know. (*She does—but fumbles now and then. Her fine movements are little better*)

Philip Today, I've seen them all, Doctor Davidson, the social worker, discussed rehabilitation with Mr Ward, the lot! They're all pleased. They say I've done well.

Philip takes his own pieces, and in due course they begin to play, if in a desultory fashion—their attention really on their conversation

Kathy You have.

Philip Only on their terms. When I leave, it's physiotherapy as an out-patient at the local hospital, three mornings a week.

Kathy How long for?

Philip I said how many weeks or months, because I've got to make a living. They said it might be wiser to think in terms of a year . . . or two . . . it would depend. "Depend on what?" "Well, any improvement will be slower now . . . it depends . . ." I gave up. But my old life, can't go back to that yet. I'll be having treatment. If you're not available, your name's soon forgotten in my business.

Kathy Is there some . . . different job you could do?

Philip Writing's the only trade I know.

Kathy You could write a . . . story . . . a novel . . . have it made into a film.

Philip I could win the football pools too, the chances are about the same. Kathy, most novelists have another job, their books earn practically nothing.

Kathy Some make a lot.

Philip Very few.

Kathy You might be one of them.
Philip I've never written fiction.
Kathy No one ever has ... until they try.
Philip Did you nag your fellow to death about where to drill for oil?
Kathy I didn't care about oil ... I do care about words.
Philip My flat's not paid for. I have to settle for what I can get, not day-dream about a novel which'd take a year to do with nothing coming in. Even if I knew what to write about, which I don't.
Kathy You could think of something.
Philip What? Tell me, come on. (*Ironically*) This place?
Kathy You're the writer ...
Philip Well, one day, perhaps, who knows. Meantime ...
Kathy And I don't nag. I make ... sensible suggestions.
Philip Meantime, I've been phoning around, hustling for work.
Kathy Did you manage to ... sell your self?
Philip You make it sound like soliciting.
Kathy You know I often use the ... wrong words.
Philip You sometimes find the right ones too. Anyway, I worked my way down through the polite noises "Sure. Bear you in mind, old chap." All that. Finally got to a publisher I've met casually at various parties ...
Kathy Which publisher? Who?
Philip Don't get excited. You've never heard of him. He doesn't do novels. I doubt if he can even read. He shoves out down-market pop biographies. You know, my own amazing story, words by courtesy of writer with bank manager on his back.
Kathy Like you.
Philip A commission to do one about some racing driver. It's just research, talking to him, and then jazz it up. But there's up-front money to con my bank manager I'm back in business.
Kathy You could make it good.
Philip Good? He doesn't want it good. It's formula stuff. But if the result's OK, there could be more in the pipeline.
Kathy It's work. It's money.
Philip I know. It's only to see me through until I'm fit enough to get back to what I'm good at ... in a year or two. It feels like going backwards, that's all.
Kathy It's something. Compared with ... nothing ... it is better.
Philip I know.
Kathy I've decided.

Philip assumes Kathy means about her next move

Philip Well, put them down.
Kathy About the Play School.
Philip Oh?
Kathy I thought, and ... I've accepted ... the idea.
Philip Well, it's up to you.
Kathy I must be ... practical. You think ... I'm wrong.
Philip It's not for me to say. Your move.

Kathy I can't go back to teaching.

Philip Yet. Not yet.

Kathy I've clung to that ... "not yet" I've tried, Philip ...

Philip I know you have.

Kathy Tried until I'm ... tired ... I'm sorry if I ... disappoint you.

Philip I didn't say that.

Kathy Your face says it.

Philip Oh, Kathy ... look, we've all been through the hospital bit, but that's not the hard part. You're being treated, clever people who know what they're doing, somehow it's easy to be determined to fight and go on fighting then until you're completely recovered. It seems quite simple.

Kathy But later, it is less easy.

Philip When weeks turn into months and the sudden recovery you're hoping for doesn't happen. But there is progress, Kathy. Look back. You can measure it.

Kathy pushes her pieces away

Kathy I don't want to play.

Philip Not enough progress for you, but that's good. That's what keeps us going, as long as it's not enough.

Kathy Is that will-power ... or self-delusion?

Philip It doesn't matter. We need it. It's all we've got.

Kathy The time must come to face ... reality.

Philip What is reality?

Kathy Look around you.

Philip It doesn't end here.

Kathy You've improved more than anyone ... Tony and Douglas, they envy you ...

Philip All right, compared with them, I'm lucky ...

Kathy But even you can't go back to your real work.

Philip For the time being.

Kathy But you think you will.

Philip It's like a marathon. Perhaps twenty six miles is beyond you, but if you give up after one mile, you'll never know if you could have made five or ten or fifteen or twenty, or what.

Kathy (*stung*) Give up? Give up? You say to me about giving up?

Philip Calm down. All I meant was ...

Kathy (*interrupting*) I have not given up!

Philip Good.

Kathy I have taken a job I don't want. So have you!

Philip You're right.

Kathy Yes, I am.

Philip We've both had to compromise.

Kathy Both. So don't ... lecture me.

Philip You haven't tried the alphabet lately.

Kathy I've stopped.

Philip Why?

Kathy Because I can't.

Philip How do you know?
Kathy It is something . . . I can't do.
Philip If you've stopped trying, how do you know that?
Kathy I have tried a hundred times.
Philip Try again.
Kathy Can you run across this room . . . without your stick?
Philip No.
Kathy No!
Philip But if that's what you want . . .

Philip uses his stick to stand up and then throws it across the room. He wobbles and is on the verge of falling

Kathy quickly moves to him and restrains him, also supporting him by holding his arms

Kathy No. You'd fall down and hurt yourself.
Philip I know.
Kathy Philip, when I cannot say the alphabet . . . it hurts me.
Philip Just see how far you can get, Kathy, that's all.
Kathy Now you are nagging . . . much worse than me.
Philip When men do it, it's called encouragement for your own good.
Kathy Sit down.
Philip When I've heard you.
Kathy (*reluctantly*) All right. (*With no great enthusiasm*) A . . .B . . . C . . . . .D . .E . .F . . . . .G . .H . .I . . . . .J . .K . .L . . . .L . . . . . (*Concentrating now, Kathy moves to and fro a little, deep in her effort*)

Philip watches her, silently urging her on

. . .L . .M . .N . . . . . .O . . .P . . .Q . . . . . .R . . .S . .T . .T . . . . . .U . . .V . . . . . . U . . .V . . .W . . . . . .W . . . . . .W . . . . . .X . .X . . .Y . . . . . .Z . . .Z! (*She executes a tiny dance of triumph, flings her arms round Philip, and hugs him*) Philip, I did it!
Philip Wonderful, Kathy.
Kathy I did it! (*She kisses Philip's cheek*)
Philip Bloody wonderful.

Philip kisses Kathy back. Somehow, it lands on her lips, if lightly. They hesitate, try it again experimentally. Then they settle down to a genuine clinch. Finally, Kathy draws back from Philip, studying his face, seriously. Philip is now more or less unsupported. He staggers, reels off balance, and sits down with a bump on the coffee table

Bloody hell . . .
Kathy Are you all right?
Philip Forgot I still can't stand up on my own. Sorry.

Kathy kneels in front of him. Philip takes her hands

Philip I wouldn't have got far if you'd let me try and run.
Kathy I think you were . . . bluffing.

Philip I was bluffing. But you did it.
Kathy Yes, I did it.

Philip lightly touches her face

Philip Where do we go from here?
Kathy It was just a kiss.
Philip What does that mean?
Kathy I don't know. (*She gets up and moves away*)
Philip Kathy, please. Tell me.

Kathy is beginning to be able to formulate more complex thought patterns in speech, but it is still a struggle for her

Kathy Before this ... I knew ... myself ... what I was. A teacher. A woman. It was good ... I liked ... what I was. Now, it is ... not the same. I have lost ... things. Reading... is hard ... I cannot write ... properly ... cannot speak ... properly ... cannot teach ... the children. Before this ... I was glad ... being a woman ... it was good. Now ... I look down ... I hide ... not you, other people. They say ... I could improve ... but sometimes ... at night ... I think ... things ... if ... I do not improve, because ... the world is ... full of other people ... and ... I am afraid. No. I have not said ... what is here. (*Indicating her head*)
Philip You manage better than you realize. The most important thing, is it really all about Sam, still?
Kathy Perhaps, but ... not in that way. Of how he changed ... how he was ... before this ... and now.
Philip Kathy, I look back too, you know. But we can mourn the past all we like, it won't come back. We both have a life to live, now. I didn't know you then. You didn't know me then, we only know each other as we are now—I need you, Kathy!

They become aware that the Nurse is wheeling the hunched figure of Kevin in

Nurse Where is everyone?
Philip Watching television, I think.

The Nurse parks Kevin in his former position, back to the audience

Let's talk somewhere else.
Kathy No ... talk does not help ... not to be afraid ...
Philip Kathy—
Kathy No. Please. It's no use. You know it. I know it.

Kathy goes

The Nurse returns Philip's stick to him

Philip Mary. You must have seen hundreds of us come and go, people like me, and Kathy, and Tony, and Douglas ... what are our chances?
Nurse You'll go on improving, I expect.
Philip I mean getting better.

Nurse You're all better than you were.

Philip To me getting better means being as I was before.

Nurse Philip, I'm not a doctor. Speak to your consultant about it.

Philip He talks about coming to terms with a degree of disability. He's a pessimist. He thought I'd need a splint for my left leg. It was made. I've never used it. He's not infallible. He can be wrong.

Nurse I'm sure he was delighted you didn't need it.

Philip Oh, yes, I'm his prize patient. That is not my ambition in life, to be a neuro-surgeon's prize patient. (*His frustration and anger at fate surface*) Dear God, Mary, they're giving people new hearts, we're always hearing about the miracle of high tech medicine, where is it? I just want to walk. Appliances; crutches; sticks; wheelchairs? Doctor Davidson tells me he's been trying to get extra wash-basins installed for seven years—wash-basins! We've become a category. Food for politicians' cant, the daily dose of "compassion" for the afflicted. What do they think we are? A different species? The only thing different about us is that we got ill, or had an accident. (*He runs out of steam*)

Nurse Well, I expect you feel better after that.

Philip (*levelly*) Has anyone who's been through this place ever made a full recovery?

Nurse Most recover to some extent.

Philip Mary, it was a very simple question. Can't you give a simple answer?

Nurse There isn't one. All our patients are neurological cases who've suffered damage to the central nervous system. Most come here when the exact degree of recovery can't be predicted ...

Philip (*interrupting*) Never mind, Mary, I've heard it all before. Leave it.

Philip limps to the door and goes

The Nurse speaks, as it were, to herself rather than Kevin

Nurse Sorry, Philip, there are no miracles here, and all the will-power in the world won't make nerves regenerate. If only it would. (*To Kevin directly*) Perhaps you'd rather be in the television room with the others. Would you like that, Kevin?

There is no movement or sign from Kevin, but the Nurse crosses to the door to the TV room and opens it anyway

The idiot sound from the goggle box surges in

The Nurse returns to Kevin, and wheels him towards the television room

The Lights fade to Black-out

PROLOGUE TO SCENE 6

Dialogue from loudspeakers

Tony Like leaving school, isn't it. Everyone swears they'll keep in touch, but they won't.

Kathy No.

Tony You'll be seeing Phil though, I suppose.

Kathy I don't think so.

Tony I thought you two were getting it together.

Kathy No.

Tony Funny. Looked like it to me.

Kathy I have to be sensible ... about things ... the work I can do ... everything ... the future ... what might happen ...

Tony That's the idea. Look on the black side. Can't beat it. If I'd known about the future, I'd never have got married and had kids. Hey Kathy, you're on to something, though, I could have been screwing around all these years, if only I'd worried more about the future.

SCENE 6

Gymnasium. 9.40 a.m. Friday. The last week

Tony is parked in his wheelchair, doing the Telegraph *crossword puzzle*

Philip comes in

Tony Well, you've managed to escape then.

Philip Yes. Have to manage on my own now.

Tony Len and Doug going too. Room Six won't be the same. Have to start breaking in three new boys on Monday. I hope one of them's good at crosswords, that's all, or I'll never get the thing finished.

Philip Do you know how much longer you'll be here?

Tony Another two weeks. But they're going to recall me in three or four months time ... have another bash.

Philip Well, good luck, Tony.

Tony And you, mate.

Philip And thanks for all the bad jokes. You've made this place a bit more bearable than it might have been.

Tony Well, someone's got to have a go, Phil. (*And suddenly, his face is dead, the mask of fun gone*) It'd be bloody suicide time without a few laughs now and then. Not that there's one hell of a lot to laugh about.

Philip Not a lot, no.

Tony My firm have fixed me up with a job in the sales office until I come back here. A lot less money, though. Have to think about selling the house, I suppose. Don't really want to do that. I've worked my socks off for the place we've got. Maybe I'll try and hang on until I'm recalled.

Philip They must think there could be some further improvement.

Tony That's right. Even if it was only ten lousy steps. Cooped up in an office for good ... Jesus ... I can't stand being inside, never could.

Philip Is that where you were yesterday? Seeing your boss?

Tony No, that was something else. More of life's rich texture. On top of my bladder problems ... it's affected my sex life.

Philip I had the impression that side was all right.

Tony I kept saying it was, didn't I. Well, it's not. Talking about it, I thought
... I don't know what I thought ... that it'd come back, I suppose, a
millimetre a day, or a centimetre a month, whatever it is. ...

Philip It could be just that, a matter of time.

Tony My doctor referred me to a specialist in such things. That's where I
was. I said to him. "Just because I'm paraplegic, the other doesn't follow
does it?" He said, "No, not necessarily. It depends."

Philip Everything always does. They'd be lost without that word.

Tony Yes. They'd have to give a straight answer. They'd blow a fuse.

Philip Did you get one?

Tony They're quick on their feet, these lads. Couldn't pin him down. He
told me to do this, try that, wait for a while, and go and see him again. I
reckon that means he thinks there's a chance though, don't you?

Philip Sounds like it.

Tony The bit about waiting ... time as you said ...

Philip Time and chance, as the preacher said.

Tony Who?

Philip Ecclesiastes. "I returned, and saw under the sun, that the race is not
to the swift, nor the battle to the strong, neither yet bread to the wise, nor
yet riches to men of understanding, nor yet favour to men of skill; but
time and chance happeneth to them all."

Tony I just hope it's not too long before it "happeneth" to me that's all! My
wife's only thirty three. Can't expect her to wait for ever. She's only
human.

Philip Come on, give her a bit more credit than that. If it's a good marriage,
she'll understand.

Tony When we got married, mate, I wasn't in a bloody wheelchair. Why if it
isn't the good captain come to inspect the troops on passing out parade.

*This last because Douglas has come in with Len. Douglas walks evenly now,
but with a slow, measured pace*

Hey, Len. Great questions of history. Who said "What the *fuck* was
that?" The Lord Mayor of Hiroshima.

Douglas and Len cross, fetch their stools, and place them in position

Douglas I've never known anyone with such appalling bad taste.

Tony His lips twitched, Len. He smiled.

Kathy comes in

Philip takes a stool across to her

Douglas I most certainly did not.

Tony Come on, Doug. You'll miss me. Admit it.

Douglas Approximately the way I'd miss a dentist's drill.

Tony I've heard that one. It's bliss when it stops.

Douglas Exactly.

Tony He made a funny, Len.

Len When?

Tony Then, Len. Oh, I'm in top form today. (*He bends over his* Telegraph)

Kathy and Philip smile at each other in a private kind of way. They touch hands briefly, as if saying goodbye: speak quietly

Philip I've ordered my taxi for four thirty. Do my packing at lunch time, so in case I don't see you . . .

Kathy I've packed most of . . . my things . . . already . . . because . . .

Philip You can't wait. Me too. I've had enough! Well . . .

Philip hands Kathy the pen she admired in Act I, Scene 3. He turns away

Kathy (*as Philip moves away*) No . . . take me with you . . . will you? . . . Philip, let's try . . . shall we?

Philip Yes, of course.

Kathy I wonder how . . . it will be . . . outside.

Philip Nothing we can't deal with, the two of us. Put together, I suppose we make one more or less complete human being.

The Physiotherapist comes in, having started the music of The Floral Dance

Physiotherapist Right. It's the last day for some of you. Who'd like to take over, and give me a rest?

Tony Doug'll do it. Come on, Doug.

Physiotherapist Douglas?

Douglas No.

Tony Chicken.

Physiotherapist (*addressing unseen patients*) Andrew? Margaret? . . . come on someone . . . you all think it's so easy . . . Philip? . . . how about you?

Tony Yes, get on up there, Phil.

Philip Kathy's much better than I am.

Kathy No . . . please . . .

Tony Don't let the side down, Phil. Come on, mate. For the honour of Room Six. Rah rah rah.

Philip Yes, all right.

Tony Hooray. Give the man a big hand, folks.

Philip walks to the stool at the front and sits on it

Philip My mind's gone blank.

Tony So what's different?

Philip I think this was a serious mistake.

Douglas Too late now. You volunteered.

Tony Just make it up as you go along.

The Physiotherapist stands, watching

Philip Right. Here we go. (*Rather uncertainly, standing up, he begins the movements*)

If possible, let us cheat a little with The Floral Dance. *It begins more slowly than normal, and more quietly, so that the effect is a little funereal and*

downbeat. Very slowly and imperceptibly, as the scene continues, the pace quickens, the volume rises, until by the end, it is a rousing march

After a few moments. Philip begins to get the hang of it—he has after all seen it often enough. He ad libs his instructions to the others. He has to use his stick, while standing, but after a while he realizes that he can bang on the floor with it, in time to the beat, and begins to do so

By now The Floral Dance *has quickened, the beat strengthened, the intention being to generate an air of excitement. Philip's movements become more definite and assertive, until he is miming an aggressive march*

Tony (*also getting carried away*) That's the idea Phil. Get 'em going.

The Physiotherapist hands a pair of elbow crutches to Tony, and he stands up,—although of course he cannot move his feet

Meanwhile—

Philip You're not trying, Len. You were in the army. Come on. Stamp those feet. Head up. Shoulders back. Chest out.

Len stiffens. His knees rise, his arms swing, until he is marching on the spot with pride

That's it, Len. Show us how it's done. You too, Kathy. Head up. Back straight, look the world in the eye.

Kathy's head rises, her marching on the spot becomes more aggressive until she is matching Len

(*As Tony makes it to his feet*) Well done, Tony. Get your balance. Don't fall over. You're standing on your own two feet, mate. Come on, Douglas. You can do better than that. Trust that left leg. It'll carry you. Trust it. Never mind the young lions. You can see them off.

Douglas too responds, caught up in the growing rhythm of the march

Remember the old motto, Tony. *Nil carborundum.* Don't let the bastards grind you down.

Cautiously, without moving his feet, Tony begins to strike his crutches alternately on the floor, joining in the increasing stamp of feet

That's the idea. All those people out there, it's pot luck, eh Tony? Nothing more than that. Any of them, they could be here, and if they were they'd be no better than us. And we're as good as they are. All of us Any time. We're all the same.

And at the climax of The Floral Dance, *the stamping feet, the crutches, the sticks, have achieved an aggressive union*

It is a statement of pride, but more than that, of personal defiance. Defiance of whatever fate rendered them disabled; that defiance which is a necessary constituent of the courage necessary to take on that "normal" world which they will all re-enter

CURTAIN

CASE HISTORIES

Philip

A freelance journalist. Experienced considerable back pain mistakenly attributed to an old slipped disc. The pain became intense when abroad on an assignment, flew home, a tumour on the spinal chord diagnosed by a neuro-surgeon. Shortly after being hospitalized, he became paraplegic, but an operation restored movement.

After many weeks in hospital, where physiotherapy treatment was begun, he is transferred to a rehabilitation centre. At that stage, he is walking with two elbow crutches, and both legs and especially the left leg are very weak.

Both legs are considerably wasted, the left more than the right. Balance is, and remains, a problem. During the ensuing weeks, he progresses on to two sticks, and then to one stick.

When he leaves the centre, he will become a physiotherapy out-patient at his local hospital, three mornings a week. This further treatment is expected to last for one to two years.

By the end of his stay at the centre, he can walk reasonable distances with the aid of one stick, but all muscles below the waist are still weak (compared to "normal"), with the emphasis on the left leg and left hip. Even with his stick, he walks with a pronounced limp. His balance remains poor due to the weakness of the muscles concerned. When standing, his weight is "back" on his heels, and he is incapable of rising on to tiptoe unaided.

Kathy

A primary school teacher. Involved as a passenger in a serious road accident when the car left the road and turned over and over. Although strapped in and with no serious external head injuries, she suffered a lesion in the area lying in the frontal lobe anterior to the motor cortex of the brain. The lesion extends into the area which controls speech. This area is adjacent to the motor cortex which controls the arm. The results in her case, are:

(a) Expressive dysphasia; knows what she wants to say, but cannot say it.
(b) Nominal dysphasia; affects ability to name objects. Knows what "it" is, but not what it is called.
(c) Emotional lability; will, for no reason, burst into tears or start laughing. Will be very distressed. Knows what she is doing, but cannot help it. A common condition in post-Road Traffic Accident patients, for many months.
(d) The fine movements of her right hand are affected. Able to print some letters, but not to do "joined up" handwriting.
(e) Some difficulty in reading.

Her programme at the centre embraces speech therapy, occupational therapy and gymnasium.

She also suffers from a degree of depression, partly due to frustration with her condition—she is intensely anxious to return to teaching—but the ending of a previously stable relationship, also due to the accident, is a contributory factor.

During her treatment at the centre, she shows a considerable improvement in some respects. She becomes less dysphasic, her speech is considerably better, her emotional lability a temporary phase, passes, as does her depression.

But the fine movements of her right hand do not fully recover, and her degree of improvement is not as great as the target she had set herself.

She is not able to resume teaching, and accepts a job as a Helper in a Play School. She will continue to have speech therapy as an out-patient for as long as there is any significant degree of improvement.

Len

A crane driver, a widower with one married son and two grandchildren. His mind on other things—his intended marriage to a middle-aged lady—he slipped when descending the ladder from his crane, and fell on his back across some baulks of timber.

He suffered a Cauda Equina lesion affecting roots s2, 3 and 4 which control the bladder and bowels, but thus relatively spares the legs. This lesion would lead to an automatic bladder which is tense and hypertonic and contracts weakly when only a small amount of urine is present in the bladder. This leads to dribbling incontinence, and the need to pass urine is not appreciated. There is also partial damage to the lower lumbar roots. There is some weakness in the legs; he does not need aids, but he walks with something of a "sailor's roll". He has a permanent catheter. At a later stage (one year plus) a decision will be taken regarding an (irreversible) operation, when the muscle surrounding the bladder neck would be resected so that the bladder drains freely in an unrestricted way. He would then use a condom drainage appliance. Patients with external appliances are less prone to infection. He detests enemas, but the suppositories which he pleads to try "in case they work this time", do not.

Spasmodically apparently cheerful, he is receiving psychiatric treatment for depression, and goes through the motions in occupational therapy and gymnasium with no enthusiasm.

He views his daily personal necessities with a sense of self-disgust, and cannot face exposing all that to his lady friend, with whom he has broken it off.

His financial outlook is grim. His old firm can find nothing for him, and he is regarded as being too old for retraining.

His son is unwilling to offer him a permanent home. He will live alone and be cared for by the community services. Through a moment's inattention and the accident of age, he has become one of the casualties of our society.

Tony

A salesman, married with two children. Mildly ill at home with what he took to be flu, he got up in the middle of the night to go to the bathroom, where he fell on the floor, helpless, his legs useless. Taken to hospital, transverse myelitis was diagnosed.

Paraplegic and confined to a wheelchair, he is determined to recover. His time of life brings maximum financial responsibilities.

With the aid of elbow crutches he can stand, but that is all. He has bladder problems and has probably been trained to empty his bladder reflexly at fixed intervals together with manual expression.

A joker by nature, with frequent sly references to sex, he does much to lighten the atmosphere for his fellow patients. But this is a mask. What concerns him most, far more even than not resuming the life on the road which he loved, is the fact that his condition has affected his sex life. He clings to the hope that normal feeling will return, but his wife is only 33 and very attractive. Devoted to her for all his racy talk, he fears the future, what the years ahead may bring.

Douglas

A prosperous company director, married with children. An active, fit man, careful to keep himself in trim—"squash twice a week"—he was shocked when he suffered a stroke. It seemed so unfair. Why him? He has a left hemiplegia. The stroke affected his left side but, since he is right-handed, his speech is unimpaired.

On his left leg, he wears an ortholon splint—made of plastic, moulded to fit under the foot and behind the calf, worn over the sock. The splint controls his degree of foot drop, but if he walks without the splint his left toe will tend to catch on the floor. At night, he has a bed cradle, and sleeps with his left arm supported on a pillow. Lacking sensation in the affected leg, part of his problem is simply to believe that it will support his weight. Initially, he tends to "hop" off the affected leg as fast as possible—

The left arm too lacks sensation, movement is restricted, the fingers tend to curl, claw like. He must "place" his left hand where he wants it to be with his good right hand; resting it on the table when eating; lifting it when standing, being careful not to "leave it behind"; holding it in front of him when walking. The left arm feels as though it does not belong to him—as if an extra limb is present. He has become adept at dressing, eating, etc. with his right hand.

Care must be taken not to knock his left side. Without sensation, he will not know he has hurt himself. Sores may develop.

Like the others, he is determined to return to "the way he was" including driving his new Mercedes. But his fields of vision are affected, the nasal field in the left eye and the temporal field in the right eye. Thus he may bump into things on the left side.

His walking does improve, and when he leaves the centre, he walks evenly, but at a slow measured pace. "Like an old man", his own bitter comment. His left arm shows little improvment, and for all his efforts, the best that can be said is that it is no worse. He will not be able to drive again, but he is reasonably mobile.

All patients have their own private scale of the degree of recovery which is acceptable to them, and Douglas has not achieved his.

His work involved stress and pressure in a competitive environment, and there are ambitious younger men on the ladder just below him, "young lions". In his mind, he sees himself as visibly affected, slower in simple trivial ways, like walking along a corridor, while others pointedly wait for him, or waiting for a lift while colleagues use the stairs. He imagines the talk behind his back, that his illness has taken it out of him, he is not the man he was, perhaps he should retire early.

Whether his apprehensions are well founded or not is irrelevant. They are real to him.

FURNITURE AND PROPERTY LIST

ACT I

SCENE 1: The Gymnasium

On stage: Wall bars
         Stools

Off stage: Letter (**Kathy**)

Personal: **All patients:** wristbands (throughout)
         Tony: wheelchair, elbow crutches (throughout)
         Douglas: ortholon splint (throughout, apart from Act I Scene 4)
         Philip: elbow crutches (to Act I Scene 4); Card (Programme)

SCENE 2: The Speech Therapist's Office

On stage: Desk, two chairs
         Bookshelves

Personal: **Speech Therapist:** Handbag containing money

SCENE 3: Room 6, a ward

On stage: Four beds, four smallish wardrobes. *In them*: clothes and shoes
         Four bedside lockers. *In them*: keys (all), Patients' Handbook
           (Phillip's), cigarettes (Tony's)
         Wash-basin, large mirror
         "No Smoking" notice
         Low sockets for electric razor
         Small bottle of whisky (*under Philip's pillow*)

Off stage: Cassette player, bunch of flowers in cellophane (**Kathy**)
         Notebook (**Kathy**)

Personal: **Philip:** pen

SCENE 4: Physiotherapy

On stage: Wall bars
         Stools
         Mats
         Practice stairs with handrail
         Plinth
         Balance board
         Medicine ball
         Footballs

SCENE 5: The Patients' Lounge

On stage: Easy chairs
              Small (i.e. card) tables with chairs
              Coffee table
              Free standing ashtrays
              Various games, including draughts and Scrabble
              Paperback books
              Wheelchair. *In it:* **Kevin**

Offstage: Plastic cup, cassette player, poetry book (**Kathy**)
              Flowers in cellophane (**Nurse**)

Personal: **Tony:** *Daily Telegraph* and pen
              Cigarettes and lighter
              Philip: Two walking sticks (to Act II Scene 3)

ACT II

SCENE 1: Room 6

On stage: As Act I Scene 3
              Also: Bed cradles (*Tony and Douglas*)
              Ortholon splint (*On Douglas's locker*)
              Day clothes for patients, including slippers, dressing gowns
              In lockers: electric razors, wash-bags, toothbrushes, flannels, towels,
                  hairbrushes etc
              On Tony's locker: Urine bottle
              On Len's bed: Night urine bag

Off stage: Urine sample equipment on tray (**Nurse**)
              Two suppositories (**Nurse**)
              Sheets (**Nurse**)

Personal: **Kathy:** slip of paper

SCENE 2: The Patients' Lounge

On stage: As Act I Scene 5
              Financial Times

SCENE 3: The Speech Therapist's Office

On stage: As Act I Scene 2

SCENE 4: Physiotherapy

On stage: As Act I Scene 4

Personal: **Philip:** single stick

SCENE 5: Patients' Lounge

On stage: As Act I Scene 5 and Act II Scene 2

Off stage: Kevin in wheelchair (**Nurse**)

SCENE 6: The Gymnasium

On stage: As Act I Scene 1

Personal: **Tony:** *Daily Telegraph* and pen
            Philip: pen

LIGHTING PLOT

ACT I, Scene 1.   9.40 a.m.

To open: Bright interior lighting

Cue 1   The patients follow the Physiotherapist in marching on the spot   (Page 6)
Fade to Black-out

ACT I, Scene 2.   2.30 p.m.

To open: Bright interior lighting

Cue 2   **Speech Therapist:** "See you tomorrow, Kathy."   (Page 9)
Fade to Black-out

ACT I, Scene 3   5.30 p.m.

To open: Interior lighting

Cue 3   **Tony:** "Well, no, can't quite manage that. Kathy, Philip ..."   (Page 17)
Fade to Black-out

ACT I, Scene 4   10.00 a.m.

To open: Bright interior lighting

Cue 4   **Physiotherapist:** "... and PULL! ... and PUSH DOWN! ..."   (Page 22)
Fade to Black-out

ACT I, Scene 5   9.00 p.m.

To open: Interior lighting

Cue 5   **Kathy:** "You may forever tarry."   (Page 30)
Fade to Black-out

ACT II, Scene 1   7.30 a.m.

To open: Dim lighting

Cue 6   **Nurse** switches on light   (Page 32)
Bring up general lighting

Cue 7   **Philip:** "Right, let's go"   (Page 40)
Fade to Black-out

ACT II, SCENE 2   9.30 p.m.

To open: Interior lighting

Cue 8   **Kathy** reaches out and takes Philip's hand   (Page 46)
        Fade to Black-out

ACT II, SCENE 3   2.15 p.m.

To open: Bright interior lighting

Cue 9   **Kathy:** "... it would be ... a defeat"   (Page 48)
        Fade to Black-out

ACT II, SCENE 4   3.30 p.m.

To open: Bright interior lighting

Cue 10   **Physiotherapist:** "... push your bottom forward."   (Page 53)
         Fade to Black-out

ACT II, SCENE 5   6.45 p.m.

To open: Interior lighting

Cue 11   The **Nurse** wheels Kevin towards the television room   (Page 59)
         Fade to Black-out

ACT II, SCENE 6   9.40 a.m.

To open: Bright interior lighting

Cue 12   At the climax of *The Floral Dance*, when ready   (Page 63)
         Black-out

EFFECTS PLOT

See note on p iv.

Cue 1	When ready *Prologue to Scene 1**	(Page vi)
Cue 2	**Tony:** "Addled her brains." *Music—Trini Lopez singing* If I had a Hammer	(Page 4)
Cue 3	The patients are seated, when ready *Music finishes*	(Page 5)
Cue 4	**Kathy** smiles and faces front *Music—Brass band playing* The Floral Dance	(Page 5)
Cue 5	The patients follow the **Physiotherapist** in marching on the spot. Lights fade *Fade music*	(Page 6)
Cue 6	In Black-out, when ready *Prologue to Scene 2**	(Page 6)
Cue 7	In Black-out, when ready *Prologue to Scene 3**	(Page 10)
Cue 7a	**Douglas:** "Would you mind?" *Cassette playing voice of Speech Therapist*	(Page 11)
Cue 7b	**Kathy** moves to her own room *Fade cassette voice*	(Page 11)
Cue 8	In Black-out, when ready *Prologue to Scene 4**	(Page 17)
Cue 9	In Black-out, when ready *Prologue to Scene 5**	(Page 22)
Cue 10	To open Scene 5 *Noise of television off, cut when ready*	(Page 23)
Cue 10a	**Kathy** enters *Cassette plays the alphabet quietly*	(Page 23)
Cue 10b	**Kathy** switches off cassette player *Cut alphabet recital*	(Page 25)

ACT II

Cue 11	When ready *Prologue to Scene 1**	(Page 31)

Cue 12	In Black-out, when ready *Prologue to Scene 2**	(Page 40)
Cue 13	As Scene 2 begins *Door slam*	(Page 40)
Cue 14	In Black-out, when ready *Prologue to Scene 3**	(Page 46)
Cue 15	In Black-out, when ready *Prologue to Scene 4**	(Page 48)
Cue 16	In Black-out, when ready *Prologue to Scene 5**	(Page 53)
Cue 17	**Nurse** opens door of TV room *Noise of television off*	(Page 59)
Cue 18	The **Nurse** wheels Kevin towards the TV room, lights fade *Fade sound of television*	(Page 59)
Cue 19	In Black-out, when ready *Prologue to Scene 6**	(Page 59)
Cue 20	**Philip:** ". . . one more or less complete human being." *Music*—The Floral Dance	(Page 62)
Cue 21	At the climax of The Floral Dance, simultaneously with blackout *Cut music*	(Page 63)

**See Production Note*

Cues 7a, 7b, 10a and 10b can be "live" cassette recordings

MADE AND PRINTED IN GREAT BRITAIN BY
LATIMER TREND & COMPANY LTD PLYMOUTH

MADE IN ENGLAND